O Worship the King

O Worship the King

* * *

Services in Song

By

ZULA EVELYN COON

O worship the King, all-glorious above,
O gratefully sing His power and His love.

BROADMAN PRESS

Nashville, Tennessee

Copyright, 1951
BROADMAN PRESS
Nashville, Tennessee

Printed in the United States of America

3. F502

Dedicated

to

THE MEMORY OF MY MOTHER

WHOSE BRAVE AND BEAUTIFUL LIFE

FIRST TAUGHT ME

TO

"WORSHIP THE KING"

v

ACKNOWLEDGMENTS

I wish to acknowledge my indebtedness and gratitude to all those who have contributed in any way toward the preparation of this collection of services in song.

I wish to express deep gratitude to Virginia Ely for reading the manuscript and for her many constructive suggestions; to Mayme Hamlett and Leona Tucker for literary criticism; and to Ethel Shipley Coon for assistance in the preparation of the material.

My sincere appreciation is hereby expressed to Dr. W. Hines Sims for supervising the final work in preparation for its publication and to Dr. B. B. McKinney for his interest and encouragement.

Grateful acknowledgment is made to all authors and publishers who have so graciously given permission to use their materials. Every effort possible has been made to trace ownership, to secure permission, and to give proper credit for the use of all copyrighted materials; if there has been any infringement in this regard, it will be gladly corrected in future editions.

CONTENTS

PART III

SERVICES IN SONG FOR CHOIR USE

PART IV

VARIED USES OF HYMNS

APPENDICES

INTRODUCTION

This collection of worship services in song has grown out of a deepening interest in and a dedication to the ministry of music. Through years of teaching vocal music to college youth, a conviction has grown in the mind of the author that individuals can be touched and challenged for Christ through the medium of sacred song as readily as they can be reached by the spoken word.

From biblical times even down to the present, Christianity has always been a singing movement. Even as music has been a mighty force in teaching religious truth in the past, so it remains today. Truth in the language of a hymn will readily implant itself in the plastic mind of youth and will deepen in meaning as life goes on to broader and richer Christian experience. It may have a rich and powerful influence upon the molding of life and character and contribute much toward leading one to live a more noble and Christ-like life.

Consider the way in which music adapts itself to the elements of worship and gives added meaning to the bringing of money, self, and service to God. Praise and prayer are expressed again and again through the great hymns of the ages; other emotions which may be expressed through them are adoration and thanksgiving, childlike trust, loyal service, and tender devotion. There are also emotions growing out of human relationships, such as fellowship with other Christians, a desire for the salvation of those who are lost, and an ever-enlarging interest in Christ's world-encompassing program of redemption. All of these are worthy emotions which need development and expression in the life of a Christian; and music can play a large part in contributing to this development and expression.

The great body of hymnic literature has come down to us as a heritage from great souls of the past who have sought to express the deepest religious aspirations and emotions of their hearts in the words now sung by Christian congregations as a part of every worship service. And yet too frequently we hear these words sung half-heartedly, with little spirit or thought given to the challenge, the comfort, the devotion, or the praise which they seek to express. The difficulty in the average church is that there has been a too limited acquaintance with hymns and a lack of interest in and study of the rich store of hymnody which is within the reach of all. Someone has said that the average church, if it should take stock of the hymns used in its various services, would usually find few more than twenty-five hymns in its repertoire. This is bound to result in a dull, listless song service, which will inevitably lessen the interest of people, especially young people, in the services of the church. On the other hand, if the variety and uses of hymns are increased, youth and adults alike will find a deepening interest, not only in the great religious music within their reach, but also in the institution which sponsors the use of such music.

Another defect to be found in many song services, especially those for young people, is the use of an inferior type of music, more related to "jazz" than to worship, and unworthy from the standpoint both of Christian ideals and of good music standards. While youth responds to the rhythmical in music and many fine youth hymns possess striking rhythms, care must be taken, in seeking to supply rhythmic emphasis, not to resort to the use of the less dignified and sensuous waltz and syncopated rhythms, which border on the jazz type of music, and which, as someone has said, have more appeal to the heels than to the heart. This type of music has many harmful effects. Jazz music strains voices; it brings about imperfectly formed ideals as to what constitutes good rhythm and harmony; and it sadly violates the appreciation of the beautiful in music.

If such music has had a hold upon a group, it will require patient, tactful, and understanding leadership in carefully guiding them to an appreciation of the best in sacred song. Wise leaders will ever keep in mind that people need to be lifted, challenged, and strengthened by music as well as by teaching and sermon. So, in the choosing of a hymn, the leader should consider whether the one chosen is worth while from the standpoint of good poetry and good music, and whether the singing of it will contribute to the enrichment and strengthening of the lives of those who sing. He should choose only those that will create a worshipful atmosphere and will challenge and inspire the mind and spirit of the age group he is leading.

Realizing the truth of these statements, the author presents these services in song as one means by which the conditions here stated may be remedied. In this collection many of the fine worship hymns of the church, as well as the better type of gospel songs, have been utilized far more freely than in the average worship service, and the author has sought to make them an integral part of the central theme of each service.[1] While it is preferable to sing all the stanzas of a hymn when it is being used for general worship, in the case of some of these services only those stanzas have been suggested which fit most perfectly the thought to be conveyed in that part of the service in which each is to be used. The *words* of the hymns are all-important in these services; if sung with sincerity, with thoughtful attention to the message they contain, they should contribute fully as much, if not more, to the worship experience as any other worship material. Therein lies the value of group participation in the singing of as many of the hymns as possible.

It is the author's purpose that there shall be flexibility in the use of these services. Many variations may be made in order to adapt them to the equipment, needs, and abilities of the group using them. If any of the services should prove too long for the time available, this can be remedied in most cases by the omission of some of the material. Other hymns and gospel songs may be substituted for those suggested; some may be rendered as solos or by small ensemble groups, even though not designated as such. The reading of the words to a musical background of the hymn tune may be used occasionally to augment the message which the hymn holds for the worshiper. In many cases, more than one hymn has been suggested so that if one is unfamiliar to the group participating, the other may be substituted. However, a number of hymns have been introduced which are not widely used by the majority of congregations, with the hope that these very worthwhile hymns might be learned and added to the body of hymns used for worship purposes.

If the worship leader does not care to use the prayers suggested in some of the services, the thought of the prayer, if not the exact wording, may be utilized by the one who leads the prayer.

---

1. The term "hymn" has been used throughout the entire collection of services to indicate both hymn and gospel song.

While some of these services have been developed for and used with young people's groups, the majority of them may be adapted to adult or other age groups. Types of services in which they may be used will include worship assemblies of various kinds—prayer meeting groups, vesper services, outdoor meetings, and other gatherings.

The following suggestions are made to insure a smooth presentation of each service. Before the service begins, the leader will explain briefly the plan of the service: that it is to be a worship service in song; that the message contained in the words of the hymns is to be as much a part of the devotional thought and theme as any other part of the service; that the hymns are to be sung without announcement, by all participating, and that the signal to sing will be given by a single chord on the piano. (A brief prelude may be preferred to introduce each hymn.)

The names of the hymns to be used may be placed on a blackboard which all can see, with the number indicated in the hymnal, the number of stanzas to be sung, and in some cases, the words; or they may be given out to the group on mimeographed or typewritten sheets of paper. This avoids the necessity of announcements, which detract from the continuity and worship atmosphere of the service.

The success of these worship services will depend much upon the way in which the accompanist enters into his part of the service. The pianist or organist should be fully informed beforehand concerning the nature of the service and of his part in it. He should have a written outline of the program, with the exact order of the hymns, musical numbers, and stanzas to be sung. Usually a nod by the leader will indicate to the accompanist that it is time for the next hymn, which he can then introduce with a chord or brief introduction on piano or organ. In the more elaborate services, careful rehearsing on the part of accompanist and the other participants before the service will be necessary in order to insure a smooth rendition.

A word should be added concerning the spirit and character of the accompaniments. An accompanist can either create or destroy an atmosphere of worship by the type of playing which he does.

xiv

He should understand that *spirit* as well as *technique* is essential to the interpretation of worship music, and play the hymns and musical numbers in a way which will help to secure the desired spiritual response on the part of the worshipers. This will eliminate all "showmanship" on his part, all efforts to magnify his "performance" above that of the singers, all "musical gymnastics" which detract from rather than create a spirit of worship. The "Musical Meditation" periods are especially designed to produce an atmosphere conducive to worship. A proper appreciation and interpretation of the message of each musical number with full, rich harmonies and artistic musical rendition will enhance each number so as to make the singing of it a real worship experience.

The first three parts of this collection contain planned worship services, (1) for general use, (2) for special occasions, such as religious holidays, etc., and (3) for choir use. Part I is divided into three sections, with an introductory explanation at the beginning of each section. The division in this case has been made on a time basis.

Part IV does not contain fully planned programs but rather presents an array of other possibilities for using hymns in worship services in order to lend variety and interest to the services.

A worship leader should be constantly on the alert to add variety to the worship periods for which he is responsible. There should be variety in the type of program used, not using the same pattern for each service. A program in which music predominates should not characterize every service; however, occasionally such a program is desirable, and in all services music should have a prominent place. The suggestions in Part IV are given to indicate different methods by which the music portion of the worship service may be varied. The suggestions and directions given will require careful study and varied use if the intended results are to be attained. One or more examples of each different method are given, and sources for finding additional material listed. A worship or song leader, following these examples and creating others of his own, will find many possibilities for varying the use of hymns in the services which he is planning.

The author presents this book of worship services in song to all those who love to "worship the King." May every person who sings the songs presented here become more keenly aware that "music is a sacred, a divine, a God-like thing, and was given to man by Christ to lift our hearts up to God, and make us feel something of the glory and beauty of God, and of all which God has made" (Charles Kingsley).

> We thank Thee, our Father, for all things beautiful. Open our minds to the beauty that is Music, and teach us to remember it as a part of Thy great goodness to us. Help us to grow each day unto the stature of Thy grace, and keep our hearts so tuned with Thy heart, that our lives may resound Thy very music, in the melody of lovely living, and in service that is song.
>
> —AUTHOR UNKNOWN

I AM MUSIC

Servant and master am I; servant of those dead, and master of those living. Through me spirits immortal speak the message that makes the world weep, and laugh, and wonder, and worship.

I tell the story of love and the story of hate; the story that saves, and the story that damns. I am the incense upon which prayers float to Heaven. I am the smoke which palls over the field of battle where men lie dying with me on their lips.

I am close to the marriage altar, and when the grave opens I stand nearby. I call the wanderer home, I rescue the soul from the depths, I open the lips of lovers, and through me the dead whisper to the living.

One I serve as I serve all; and the king I make my slave as easily as I subject his slave. I speak through the birds of the air, the insects of the field, the crash of waters on rock-ribbed shores, the sighing of wind in the trees, and I am even heard by the soul that knows me in the clatter of wheels on city streets.

I know no brother, yet all men are my brothers; I am the father of the best that is in them, and they are the fathers of the best that is in me; I am of them, and they are of me; for I am the instrument of God. I AM MUSIC.

—AUTHOR UNKNOWN

PART I

SERVICES IN SONG
FOR
GENERAL OCCASIONS

SECTION I

The services in this section are for use in Sunday school assemblies, young people's prayer meetings, and similar gatherings, where a fifteen- to twenty-minute period is available.

SERVICE 1

"IN THE BEGINNING, GOD . . ."

MUSICAL MEDITATION: "He Leadeth Me," or
"In Heavenly Love Abiding"

LEADER:

There are just two ways in which one can begin a journey. One way is to begin it by learning all you possibly can from those who have traveled the way before you, or by using a guidebook or a road map which has the route carefully marked out for you. The other way, which is seldom used, is to start on your journey without information of any kind, in which case you must trust chance alone to find the way to your destination and thus run the risk of losing the way entirely.

Foolish as this last way may seem, it is just the way in which many young people start out on the journey of life. Suppose I should ask each one of you, as you begin life's journey, this question, "Where are you going, Youth?" Would you flippantly reply, "We don't know where we're going, but we're on our way!" Or would your answer hold purpose and aspiration as you tell me what you hope your destination will be and how you plan to reach that destination which lies out beyond your youthful years?

To help you to answer this question, I give to you four bits of information from the greatest Guidebook which has ever been written, in the hope that this information will help you to chart your course and reach your destination safely. So much depends upon the way in which we start a journey—and the right beginning usually results in a "happy landing."

3

Let us first look at the very beginning of all beginnings, the one we find recorded on the first page of this Guidebook, God's Word. There we read, *"In the beginning God."*

"In the beginning God!" What better way could there be for any-one to face a new beginning? As you begin this journey of life, let us see just how this kind of a beginning will help you. From other portions of God's Word I am adding to these four words to give you the answer.

First, in the beginning God—*"leadeth* thee by the way that thou shouldest go" (Isaiah 48:17). He has traveled all the way before you, and knows just how to help you chart your journey so that you will not go astray.

> I know not what the future hath
> Of marvel or surprise,
> Assured alone that life and death
> His mercy underlies.
>
> I know not where His islands lift
> Their fronded palms in air;
> I only know I cannot drift
> Beyond His love and care.
>
> —JOHN G. WHITTIER

HYMN: "Guide Me, O Thou Great Jehovah" (stanzas 1, 2), or "He Leadeth Me" (stanza 1)

LEADER:

Second, in the beginning God—"will *instruct* thee and *teach* thee in the way which thou shalt go" (Psalm 32:8). He is the "Lord thy God which *teacheth* thee to profit" (Isaiah 48:17). You attend school in order to gain in wisdom and knowledge that you may be better equipped for the tasks of life. There you find teachers who are prepared to guide you in acquiring the knowledge which you need to possess, but unless you learn from the greatest of all teach-ers, you will not have gained the deepest knowledge and the greatest truth which life holds for you.

The Lord is my Teacher;
I shall not lose the way to wisdom.
He leadeth me in the lowly path of learning,
He prepareth a lesson for me every day.
He findeth the clear fountain of instruction—
Little by little He showeth me the beauty of truth.

The world is a great book that He has written,
He turneth the leaves for me slowly;
They are all inscribed with images and letters—
His voice poureth light on the pictures and the words.

Then am I glad when I perceive His meaning.
He taketh me by the hand to the hill-top of wisdom;
In the valley, also, He walketh beside me,
And in the dark places He whispereth in my heart.

Yea, though my lesson be hard, it is not hopeless,
For the Lord is very patient with His slow scholar.
He will wait awhile for my weakness—
He will help me to read the truth through tears—
Surely Thou wilt enlighten me daily by joy and by sorrow,
And lead me at last, O Lord, to the perfect knowledge of Thee.[1]

—HENRY VAN DYKE

HYMN: "More About Jesus" (stanzas 2, 3), or
         "Lord, Speak to Me, That I May Speak" (stanzas 1, 3)

LEADER:

Third, in the beginning God—"is a *friend* that sticketh closer than a brother" (Proverbs 18:24). There are no finer, truer friendships than those formed during high school and college days; but the truest friendship one can form is the friendship with that One who said, "Greater love hath no man than this, that a man lay down his life for his friends. Ye are my friends, if ye do whatsoever I command you" (John 15:13-14), and then went on to prove his word by laying down his life for you and for me. As you cultivate *this* friendship, your very life will be vocal with this testimony:

---

1. "The Psalm of the Good Teacher." Reprinted from *The Poems of Henry van Dyke;* copyright, 1911 by Charles Scribner's Sons, 1939 by Tertius van Dyke; used by permission of the publishers.

I've found a Friend, oh, such a Friend!
He loved me ere I knew Him;
He drew me with the cords of love,
And thus He bound me to Him.
And 'round my heart still closely twine
Those ties which naught can sever,
For I am His, and He is mine,
Forever and forever.

I've found a Friend, oh, such a Friend!
He bled, He died to save me;
And not alone the gift of life,
But His own self He gave me.
Naught that I have my own I call,
I hold it for the Giver:
My heart, my strength, my life, my all,
Are His, and His forever.

I've found a Friend, oh, such a Friend!
So kind, and true, and tender,
So wise a Counsellor and Guide,
So mighty a Defender!
From Him, who loves me now so well,
What power my soul can sever?
Shall life or death, or earth or hell?
No; I am His forever.

                                —J. G. SMALL

HYMN: "Jesus Is All the World to Me" (stanzas 1, 2, 4), or
        "What a Friend" (stanzas 1, 3)

LEADER:

Fourth, in the beginning God—"shall *supply all your need* according to his riches in glory by Christ Jesus" (Philippians 4:19). There will be needs of every kind and description during the years ahead, but let us remember that:

        All you may need He will provide,
        God will take care of you.

HYMN: "God Will Take Care of You" (stanzas 3, 4), or
        "Moment by Moment" (stanzas 2, 4)

LEADER:

So we have come to see that in the beginning of our journey of life, God will *lead* us every step of the way. He will be our greatest *Teacher,* our truest *Friend,* and will *supply all our need* through his riches in Christ Jesus.

Let us now return to our first question, "Where are you going, Youth?" Will you purpose in your hearts to make *this* your destination as you are now beginning life's journey?

> To lift Today above the Past;
> To make Tomorrow sure and fast;
> To nail God's colors to the mast?

Then—

> God go with you, Youth.[2]

HYMN: "Just As I Am, Thine Own to Be" (all stanzas), or
"Arise, O Youth of God" (all stanzas), or
"Now in the Days of Youth" (Tune: "Diademata.")

> Now in the days of youth,
> When life flows fresh and free,
> Thou Lord of all our hearts and lives,
> We give ourselves to thee;
> Our fervent gift receive,
> And fit us to fulfill,
> Through all our days, in all our ways,
> Our heavenly Father's will.
>
> Teach us where'er we live,
> To act as in thy sight,
> And do what thou wouldst have us do
> With radiant delight;
> Not choosing what is great,
> Nor spurning what is small,
> But take as from thy hands our tasks,
> And glorify them all.
>
> Teach us to love the true,
> The beautiful and pure,
> And let us not for one short hour
> An evil thought endure;
> But give us grace to stand
> Decided, brave and strong,
> The lovers of all holy things.
> The foes of all things wrong.

---

2. From the poem, "Where Are You Going, Great-Heart?" by John Oxenham. Used in slightly altered form by permission of Erica Oxenham.

Spirit of Christ, do Thou
Our first bright days inspire
That we may live the life of love
And loftiest desire;
And be by thee prepared
For larger years to come,
And for the life ineffable
Within the Father's home.[3]

—WALTER J. MATHAMS

PRAYER OF CONSECRATION (by leader):

"Our Father, we thank Thee for the springtime of life, for its freshness and beauty. We thank Thee for the enthusiasm and radiance of youth. We would that all the powers with which Thou hast endowed young men and young women might be consecrated to Thee, so that no gift might be marred, none mutilated, none lost; but that all might be kept and invested and thus enriched and multiplied in Thy service. Let the young people know of Thy loving solicitude, Thy sympathetic care, and Thine infinite wisdom for the right employment of life, and may they find in their deepest inner experience the sweetness and glory of Thy reward. For Jesus' sake. Amen."[4]

SUGGESTIONS FOR CARRYING OUT THIS SERVICE:

This service is for young people of high school or college age. While best suited for use for some "beginning," such as the beginning of a school year, it can be used in any service for young people which seeks to challenge them to commit the beginning of life to the One who can make all life purposeful and abundant. The hymns suggested may be sung by the entire group.

---

3. "Now in the Days of Youth," by Walter J. Mathams. From *New Worship and Song,* copyright, 1942 by the Pilgrim Press. Used by permission.

4. By Mrs. J. M. Dawson from *Talking with God,* edited by Alfred Franklin Smith. Copyright 1929 by Lamar & Whitmore. By permission of Abingdon-Cokesbury Press.

SERVICE 2

"I'D RATHER HAVE JESUS"[1]

HYMN: "Blessed Assurance" (group or recording)

LEADER:

> I'd rather have Jesus than silver or gold,
> I'd rather be His than have riches untold;
> I'd rather have Jesus than houses or lands,
> I'd rather be led by His nail-pierced hand,
> Than to be the king of a vast domain
> And be held in sin's dread sway;
> I'd rather have Jesus than anything
> This world affords today.

And the second verse begins, "I'd rather have Jesus than men's applause" and continues, "I'd rather have Jesus than world-wide fame" . . . sentences which struck the very heart of a young man as he sat before his piano early one Sunday morning. His mother, a minister's wife, had placed the beautiful poem where her son would see it . . . and with the prayer that he, a Christian, would become wholly consecrated in His service. She knew of the offer he was pondering of a radio contract which would give him opportunity for fame and possible riches in exchange for his regular appearance on a secular program.

It was in the thirties; business curves were still heading downward, and there was rumor of a salary cut in the downtown New York insurance office where the 22-year old singer worked as a clerk. "Radio," . . . a magic word, for had not obscure names become nationally known overnight as millions began to hear new voices and become acquainted with new personalities? Then, too, there was money to be made in radio. Beverly Shea thought on these things as he rehearsed a hymn he was to sing in church that morning.

---

1. Adapted from "The Story of a Song," by V. C. Hogren. Copyright, 1947, by Van Kampen Press. Used by permission.

His eyes again fell on the words of Mrs. Rhea Miller's poem and he read, "I'd rather have Jesus than silver or gold." His fingers unconsciously fell to the keyboard and wrote out the melody which is today known to millions. Several days later the director who spoke to Mr. Shea in behalf of the radio network was amazed to receive a firm "no" in response to his offer. "No" was a strange word to the director's ears as thousands of singers would have leaped at such an opportunity as was proposed to the young bass-baritone.

From that time forward, there was never any doubt as to the course which Mr. Shea was to pursue in full-time Christian service, and the words of the poem, "I'd Rather Have Jesus," set to music became his testimony. Wherever he appeared, he was certain to sing his earlier decision; and through the years which have followed, untold thousands have had their lives transformed through the hearing of this simple yet powerful testimony.

Today, Beverly Shea is realizing his ambition to sing the gospel on the radio. A nationally known aluminum firm, headed by a Christian man, sponsors Shea's hymn program heard by thousands each week, and he is having the joy of singing his own and other songs of testimony in the Saturday evening youth meetings of Chicago, New York, and other American and Canadian cities. Shea receives more invitations to sing in churches over the country than he can possibly accept and gives everywhere the testimony that "God can guide young lives when we give the direction over to him, and 'no good thing will he withhold. . . .' " The familiar verse Shea likes to attach to his signature is found in Psalm 71:23: "My lips shall greatly rejoice when I sing unto thee; and my soul, which thou hast redeemed."

HYMN: "I'd Rather Have Jesus" (solo or recording)

STORY:

A lonely sailor wandered into a gaudy night club in Philadelphia . . . attracted by the crowd and its laughter. A radio blared, and its sound was in keeping with the forced gaiety beyond the open doors. The program stopped, the usual time signal was given, a spot announcement or two followed. Another program came on, to which no one in the club seemed to pay much attention. Then a deep melodious voice sang, "I'd rather have Jesus than anything this world affords today."

Two weeks later, this same sailor walked down Philadelphia's Broad Street, and with a smile he stopped another bluejacket who carried a large Bible under his arm. The first sailor pulled a small New Testament from his pocket as he said, "Mine's not as big, and I haven't had it long either. Just two weeks ago I was in a place I shouldn't have been. There was a radio going, and after awhile I heard a fellow singing a song I couldn't get away from. It was, 'I'd rather have Jesus than anything this world could offer.' When the song was over, a chap on the radio started telling about giving the heart to Jesus and forsaking a life of sin. I got out of that place and went around the corner to the Christian Service Center. There they gave me this Testament and led me to Christ."

It was Beverly Shea's voice the sailor heard that night.

HYMN: "I'd Rather Have Jesus" (stanza 1, sung by group)

STORY:

An actress on Broadway chanced to tune in the Saturday night radio program of Jack Wyrtzen. Her letter follows:

"While backstage in my dressing room in a theater off Broadway, I happened to have turned on the radio and recognized your opening hymn, 'Wonderful Words of Life.' It was a great inspiration to me. A year and a half ago I thought I was the happiest person in the universe when I was offered a position on the stage. My mother, being saved, objected to this, but having a stubborn streak in me, I signed a contract with the agent and on the stage I went. As I said before, I thought I was the happiest person since I had everything my heart desired—money, clothes, the so-called good times. Everything went fine for a half year, but within the past year I've been living in misery. I thought I'd escape this by going to Hollywood, but my greatest misery took place there; so I returned to New York. If you were to ask me what I remembered on your broadcast, I would have to say nothing, except the following words, 'Choose you this day whom you will serve.' Just before curtain

time these words were ringing in my ears. When I was told to be
ready to go on in three minutes, a fear came over me. Out of all
the lines I had memorized, I could think of none but 'Choose you
this day whom you will serve.' That night, instead of going with
the rest of the actors and actresses, I went home, wanting to get
away from it all. I didn't mean to trouble you with my troubles,
but I wish you would pray for me. I would appreciate it if you would
sing a song I've heard but once—'I'd Rather Have Jesus.' I'm
thanking you and looking forward to this Saturday night."

HYMN: "I'd Rather Have Jesus" (stanza 2, sung by group)

STORY:

During their trip to the United States, the King and Queen of
England were spending an evening with President and Mrs. Roose-
velt. Chief Whitefeather, grandson of Sitting Bull, was asked to
entertain. One of his songs was, "I'd Rather Have Jesus." When
he finished, King George is reported to have said, "That's my
testimony, too."

A thousand grim marines sat on a South Pacific isle listening to
a gospel message punctuated with gunfire in the distance. When the
chaplain sat down, a marine stood to his feet to sing the closing
hymn. As the shell-scarred palms swayed near by, more than half of
that company of battle-grimed veterans came forward to take the
Lord Jesus as Saviour. The marine, a former opera singer, had
just concluded singing, "I'd rather have Jesus and let Him lead."

HYMN: "I'd Rather Have Jesus" (stanza 3, sung by group)
      (After the singing of this stanza, organ music continues
      through the concluding story.)

STORY:

Shortly after the Normandy invasion, a chaplain's assistant sat
at the organ console in one of France's famous cathedrals. The
strains of "I'd Rather Have Jesus" drifted through the windowless
edifice to reach the ears . . . and hearts of jeep riding GI's and the
French peasants as they stopped to listen. Another organ, . . . the

one used by the famous physician and concert organist, Albert Schweitzer . . . played by the same chaplain's assistant, also responded to the simple strains of "I'd Rather Have Jesus." In a letter to Beverly Shea, this soldier closed with, "I wanted you to know how wonderful I think your song is and to let you know that churches in France and Germany have heard it re-echo through their sacred walls."

LEADER:

The power of this song, which is literally sweeping America and beyond, can never be estimated. The incidents reported and the many others not recorded in this story indicate the power of a testimony which only eternity can fully evaluate . . . since that Sunday morning when a young man's life was fully surrendered as he wrote the music for a poem which was destined to touch the lives of the weak and the strong, the poor and those more fortunate, the weary and the glad . . . on far flung battlefronts, in the face of death, in the White House, in happy homes and broken ones, in shattered cathedrals and on coral strands, in tempest and in calm.

Are the words of this song *your* testimony, too? Let us bow our heads and quietly consider the claims of Jesus upon our hearts and lives in these closing moments of our meditation.

HYMN: "Softly and Tenderly" (solo, quartet or recording)

SUGGESTIONS FOR CARRYING OUT THIS SERVICE:

Recordings, sung by Beverly Shea, of all the hymns suggested for this service are available. It is preferable to use these recordings with the service if they can be secured. If not, a solo or quartet may render the songs as indicated.

Different storytellers may be used for the different stories. As many or as few of these may be used as time permits.

(See Appendix II for source of the song, "I'd Rather Have Jesus.")

SERVICE 3

CHRIST'S MEDLEY

MUSICAL MEDITATION: "Tread Softly" (Continue through following introduction.)

INTRODUCTION (by leader):

In this quiet hour of meditation, the invisible Christ stands in our midst, waiting to speak to our hearts through the voice of music. If we but listen, we shall hear a medley of melody which Christ himself created and left on printed page for our spirit's joy and comfort. The melodies are recorded for us by his beloved disciple, John. Let us listen as they are now blended into a medley of music by Christ, the master Musician.

HYMN (violin or organ): "Break Thou the Bread of Life"
(to be played throughout the following readings)

1ST READER:

"And Jesus said unto them, *I am the bread of life*: he that cometh to me shall never hunger. . . . I am the living bread which came down from heaven: if any man eat of this bread, he shall live for ever: and the bread that I will give is my flesh, which I will give for the life of the world" (John 6:35, 51).

2ND READER:

Thou art the Bread of Life,
O Lord, to me,
Thy holy Word the truth
That saveth me,
Give me to eat and live
With Thee above;
Teach me to love Thy truth,
For Thou art love.

—MARY A. LATHBURY

HYMN (violin or organ): "The Light of the World Is Jesus"
(to be played throughout the following readings)

1ST READER:

"Then spake Jesus . . . unto them, saying, *I am the light of the world*: he that followeth me shall not walk in darkness, but shall have the light of life. . . . I am come a light into the world, that whosoever believeth on me should not abide in darkness" (John 8:12; 12:46).

2ND READER:

I heard the voice of Jesus say,
"I am this dark world's Light;
Look unto me, thy morn shall rise
And all thy day be bright."
I looked to Jesus and I found
In Him, my Star, my Sun;
And in that light of life I'll walk
Till traveling days are done.

—HORATIUS BONAR

HYMN (violin or organ): "The Lord Is My Shepherd"
(to be played throughout the following readings)

1ST READER:

"Then said Jesus unto them, . . . *I am the good shepherd*: the good shepherd giveth his life for the sheep. . . . I am the good shepherd, and know my sheep, and am known of mine. As the Father knoweth me, even so know I the Father: and I lay down my life for the sheep. And other sheep I have, which are not of this fold: them also I must bring, and they shall hear my voice; and there shall be one fold, and one shepherd" (John 10:7, 11, 14-16).

2ND READER:

The King of Love my Shepherd is,
Whose goodness faileth never;
I nothing lack if I am His,
And He is mine forever.

Where streams of living water flow
My ransomed soul He leadeth,
And where the verdant pastures grow,
With food celestial feedeth.

In death's dark vale I fear no ill,
With Thee, dear Lord, beside me;
Thy rod and staff my comfort still,
Thy cross before to guide me.

And so, thro' all the length of days,
Thy goodness faileth never;
Good Shepherd, may I sing Thy praise
Within Thy house forever.
—HENRY W. BAKER

HYMN (violin or organ): "Just as I Am"
    (to be played throughout the following readings)

1ST READER:

"Jesus saith . . . *I am the way, the truth, and the life*: no man
cometh unto the Father, but by me" (John 14:6).

2ND READER:

Thou art the Way; to Thee alone
From sin and death we flee;
And he who would the Father seek,
Must seek Him, Lord, by Thee.

Thou art the Truth; Thy word alone
True wisdom can impart;
Thou only canst inform the mind,
And purify the heart.

Thou art the Life; the rending tomb
Proclaims Thy conquering arm;
And those who put their trust in Thee
Nor death nor hell shall harm.

Thou art the Way, the Truth, the Life;
Grant us that way to know,
That truth to keep, that life to win,
Whose joys eternal flow.
—G. W. DOANE

HYMN (violin or organ): "Face to Face," or
    "I Know That My Redeemer Lives" (Tune: "Messiah")
    (to be played throughout the following readings)

1ST READER:

"Jesus said . . . *I am the resurrection, and the life*: he that believeth in me, though he were dead, yet shall he live: and whosoever liveth and believeth in me shall never die" (John 11:25-26).

2ND READER:

> "I am alive forever!"
>   This is the word He said;
> In Him there is no dying,
>   In Him there are no dead;
> "I am alive forever!"—
>   This is His word to me,
> Through springtime after springtime
>   To live eternally.
>
> . . . .
>
> I know not how the future
>   Shall change me or surprise,
> But this will be my heaven,
>   To look into His eyes,
> To hear again His promise
>   As He sweetly welcomes me—
> "Thou art alive forever,
>   Alive eternally!"[1]
>
> —RALPH SPAULDING CUSHMAN

DIRECTED MEDITATION (by leader):

(Music of "I Need Thee Every Hour" played throughout first part of meditation period)

In these closing moments of our meditation, let us think of Jesus as he faced the spiritual hunger of men's souls and sang the marvelous melody of his all-sufficiency, *"I am the bread of life."* Let us pray for a hunger and thirst after righteousness which shall be filled by the living Bread of the Lord Jesus.

(Pause for silent prayer and meditation.)

Let us now think of Christ as he faced the blindness of men's minds and hearts and sang his "song in the night," *"I am the light of the world."* Let us come to the Light that we, too, may sing, "Once I was blind, but now I can see; the light of the world is Jesus."

---

1. From poem, "Alive Forever." From *Spiritual Hilltops*, by Ralph S. Cushman. Copyright, 1932, by Ralph S. Cushman. By permission of Abingdon-Cokesbury Press.

(Pause for silent prayer and meditation.)

(Music changes to "Jesus, Lover of My Soul")

Let us think of the compassion of Jesus as he saw the waywardness of his beloved sheep, and sang to them the tender melody of his shepherd heart, *"I am the good shepherd."* Let us turn our wayward feet into the paths of the Good Shepherd that he may lead us into the green pastures and beside the still waters which he has provided for those who love him.

(Pause for silent prayer and meditation.)

Let us think of the patient Jesus as he faced the misunderstanding of those nearest and dearest to him and met their bewilderment by his song of comfort and of hope, *"I am the way, the truth, and the life."* Let us ask him to teach us to walk in his way, to abide in his truth, and to live his life "till traveling days are done."

(Pause for silent prayer and meditation.)

(Music changes to "Majestic Sweetness Sits Enthroned")

Let us think of Christ, our Saviour and Redeemer, as he climaxed his Song of Redemption in the matchless Melody of his Resurrection, *"I am the resurrection, and the life."* May we bow in humble gratitude and fervent praise as we thank him for the medley of these marvelous melodies which he has sung to us out of the sacred score of his written Word.

HYMN: "Majestic Sweetness Sits Enthroned"

(Concealed soloist sings the first three stanzas; then leader gives benediction as organ continues to play the hymn through the first half of the fourth stanza; soloist then concludes by singing the last half of the fourth stanza—"He makes me triumph over death, and saves me from the grave. Amen.")

BENEDICTION:

Now unto him that is able to do exceeding abundantly above all that we ask or think, according to the power that worketh in us, unto him be glory . . . throughout all ages, world without end Ephesians 3:20-21).

SUGGESTIONS FOR CARRYING OUT THIS SERVICE:

This service is to be given with a continuous musical background of organ or violin music throughout. No songs are sung until the concluding solo. The musicians, together with readers, should rehearse carefully so that there will be no portion of the entire program where the music ceases. If the second reader concludes his reading before the accompanying hymn is finished, the first reader should wait until the next hymn begins before continuing the reading. Each hymn has been selected to fit the theme of the two readings which follow.

Use a man and a woman for the alternate readings; select those who can interpret the readings with deep feeling and appreciation. It is preferable to have all participants (readers and musicians), with the exception of the leader, concealed.

SERVICE 4

PAUL'S SYMPHONY

MUSICAL MEDITATION: "I Love to Tell the Story"

LEADER:

Can you imagine what God's Word would be if Paul, the great
apostle to the Gentiles, had failed "to tell the story of Jesus and
his love"? His words have rung out like a great, majestic symphony
to the countless millions of Christ's followers throughout the ages,
and all have found in his message a song of consolation, of guidance, and of hope.

The music which Paul has given to the world has many themes,
and yet, uniting and transcending them all is the one central, eternal
theme—the theme of the victorious Redeemer, Jesus Christ. Let us
listen to some of the themes of Paul's symphony that they may
enrich our needy hearts and set them afire once more with their
harmony and beauty.

THEME OF SALVATION (1ST READER):

"If thou shalt confess with thy mouth the Lord Jesus, and shalt
believe in thine heart that God hath raised him from the dead, thou
shalt be saved. For with the heart man believeth unto righteousness;
and with the mouth confession is made unto salvation. . . . For
whosoever shall call upon the name of the Lord shall be saved"
(Romans 10:9-10, 13).

HYMN: "Whosoever Will" (stanzas 1, 3), or
         "Sinners Jesus Will Receive" (stanzas 1, 2), or
         "I Hear Thy Welcome Voice" (stanzas 1, 3)

THEME OF CONSECRATION (2ND READER):

"I beseech you therefore, brethren, by the mercies of God, that
ye present your bodies a living sacrifice, holy, acceptable unto

God, which is your reasonable service. And be not conformed to this world: but be ye transformed by the renewing of your mind, that ye may prove what is that good, and acceptable, and perfect, will of God" (Romans 12:1-2).

HYMN: "Take My Life, and Let It Be" (stanzas 1, 4)

THEME OF THE CROSS (1ST READER):

"I am crucified with Christ: nevertheless I live; yet not I, but Christ liveth in me: and the life which I now live in the flesh I live by the faith of the Son of God, who loved me, and gave himself for me. . . . But God forbid that I should glory, save in the cross of our Lord Jesus Christ, by whom the world is crucified unto me, and I unto the world" (Galatians 2:20; 6:14).

HYMN: "In the Cross of Christ I Glory" (stanzas 1, 4)

THEME OF LOVE (2ND READER):

"If I speak with the tongues of men and of angels, but have not love, I am become sounding brass, or a clanging cymbal. And if I have the gift of prophecy, and know all mysteries and all knowledge; and if I have all faith, so as to remove mountains, but have not love, I am nothing. And if I bestow all my goods to feed the poor, and if I give my body to be burned, but have not love, it profiteth me nothing. Love suffereth long, and is kind; love envieth not; love vaunteth not itself, is not puffed up, doth not behave itself unseemly, seeketh not its own, is not provoked, taketh not account of evil; rejoiceth not in unrighteousness, but rejoiceth with the truth; beareth all things, believeth all things, hopeth all things, endureth all things. . . . But now abideth faith, hope, love, these three; and the greatest of these is love" (1 Corinthians 13:1-7, 13 ASV).

HYMN: "More Love to Thee, O Christ" (stanzas 1, 2)

THEME OF ASSURANCE AND FAITH (1ST READER):

"There hath no temptation taken you but such as is common to man: but God is faithful, who will not suffer you to be tempted above that ye are able; but will with the temptation also make a way to escape, that ye may be able to bear it" (1 Corinthians 10:13).

"For I know whom I have believed, and am persuaded that he is able to keep that which I have committed unto him against that day" (2 Timothy 1:12).

For "he said unto me, My grace is sufficient for thee: for my strength is made perfect in weakness" (2 Corinthians 12:9).

HYMN: "How Firm a Foundation" (stanzas 1, 3, 5)

THEME OF CHRISTIAN WARFARE (2ND READER):

"Put on the whole armour of God, that ye may be able to stand against the wiles of the devil. For we wrestle not against flesh and blood, but against principalities, against powers, against the rulers of the darkness of this world, against spiritual wickedness in high places. Wherefore take unto you the whole armour of God, that ye may be able to withstand in the evil day, and having done all, to stand. Stand therefore, having your loins girt about with truth, and having on the breastplate of righteousness; and your feet shod with the preparation of the gospel of peace; above all, taking the shield of faith, wherewith ye shall be able to quench all the fiery darts of the wicked. And take the helmet of salvation, and the sword of the Spirit, which is the word of God: praying always with all prayer and supplication in the Spirit, and watching thereunto with all perseverance and supplication for all saints" (Ephesians 6:11-18).

HYMN: "Stand Up, Stand Up for Jesus" (stanzas 1, 3), or
"Am I a Soldier of the Cross?" (stanzas 1, 4)

THEME OF VICTORY IN CHRIST JESUS (1ST AND 2ND READERS):

"Who shall separate us from the love of Christ? shall tribulation, or distress, or persecution, or famine, or nakedness, or peril, or sword? As it is written, For thy sake we are killed all the day long; we are accounted as sheep for the slaughter.

"Nay, in all these things we are more than conquerors through him that loved us. For I am persuaded that neither death, nor life, nor angels, nor principalities, nor powers, nor things present, nor things to come, nor height, nor depth, nor any other creature, shall be able to separate us from the love of God, which is in Christ Jesus our Lord" (Romans 8:35-39).

"But thanks be to God, which giveth us the victory through our Lord Jesus Christ" (1 Corinthians 15:57).

HYMN: "The Son of God Goes Forth to War" (stanzas 1, 4), or "Faith Is the Victory" (stanzas 1, 2)

LEADER:

Not a one of these themes may be heard without magnifying the predominant, transcendent theme of them all—the theme of Jesus Christ, the Redeemer of mankind. As we listen, their harmonies are blended and caught up into one majestic hymn of praise, whose glad message of victory rolls down through the years until it is heard in every land and on every tongue—the triumphant theme of Paul's symphony—"Jesus Saves, Jesus Saves!"

HYMN: "Jesus Saves" (stanzas 1, 3, 4)

SUGGESTIONS FOR CARRYING OUT THIS SERVICE:

This service may be used with a leader and two readers, preferably a man and a woman, who read the "themes" alternately. If a variation in the presentation of the music is desired, the hymns which follow each "theme" may be played by a violinist or by organist or pianist as a background to the Scripture reading instead of having them sung at the close of each reading. In this case, if the reader finishes reading before the hymn is ended, the next reader should not begin until his "theme" song is begun. This will link the songs definitely with the readings.

The "Theme of Victory in Christ Jesus" may be read responsively by both readers, one asking the question, "Who shall separate us from the love of Christ?" and the other answering, "Nay, in all these things we are more than conquerors." The readings would be more effective if given from memory. Choose those who can interpret the Scripture passages with sincere feeling and understanding.

SERVICE 5

IS THE MASTER SATISFIED WITH ME?

SOLO: "Satisfied with Jesus" (stanza 1 and refrain)

CALL TO WORSHIP:

"Oh that men would praise the Lord for his goodness, and for his wonderful works to the children of men! For he satisfieth the longing soul, and filleth the hungry soul with goodness" (Psalm 107:8-9).

SOLO: "Satisfied with Jesus" (refrain only)

LEADER:

Is the Master satisfied with my pleasures?

> If the soft hand of winning Pleasure leads
> By living waters, and through flowery meads,
> Where all is smiling, tranquil, and serene,
> Oh! teach me to elude each latent snare,
> And whisper to my sliding heart, "Beware."
> With caution let me hear the Syren's voice,
> And doubtful, with a trembling heart rejoice.
> If friendless in a vale of tears I stray,
> Where briars wound, and thorns perplex my way,
> Still let my steady soul Thy goodness see,
> And, with a strong confidence, lay hold on Thee.
>
> —ANNA LETITIA BARBAULD

HYMN: "In the Hour of Trial" (stanzas 1, 2)

SCRIPTURE:

"He that loveth pleasure shall be a poor man" (Proverbs 21:17). "She that liveth in pleasure is dead while she liveth" (1 Timothy

5:6). "Let not sin therefore reign in your mortal body, that ye should obey it in the lusts thereof. Neither yield ye your members as instruments of unrighteousness unto sin: but yield yourselves unto God, . . . For sin shall not have dominion over you: for ye are not under the law, but under grace" (Romans 6:12, 14). "And whatsoever ye do in word or deed, do all in the name of the Lord Jesus" (Colossians 3:17).

SOLO: "Satisfied with Jesus" (last half of refrain)

> But the question comes to me, as I think of Calvary,
> Is my Master satisfied with me?

LEADER:

Is the Master satisfied with my gifts?

> Go break to the hungry, sweet charity's bread,
> "For giving is living," the angel said.
> "Must I be giving again and again?"
> The weary, wondering question came.
> "No," said the angel, piercing me through,
> "Just give till the Master stops giving to you."

—AUTHOR UNKNOWN

HYMN: "I Gave My Life for Thee" (stanzas 1, 4), or
    "Something for Thee" (stanzas 1, 4)

SCRIPTURE:

"Thanks be unto God for his unspeakable gift" (2 Corinthians 9:15). "Our Saviour Jesus Christ . . . gave himself for us, that he might redeem us from all iniquity" (Titus 2:13-14). "Freely ye have received, freely give" (Matthew 10:8). "Every man according as he purposeth in his heart, so let him give; not grudgingly, or of necessity: for God loveth a cheerful giver" (2 Corinthians 9:7).

HYMN: "Satisfied with Jesus" (last half of refrain)

LEADER:

Is the Master satisfied with my service?

Christ has no hands but our hands
   To do His work today;
He has no feet but our feet
   To lead men in His way;
He has no tongue but our tongues
   To tell men how He died;
He has no help but our help
   To bring them to His side.

We are the only Bible
   The careless world will read;
We are the sinner's gospel,
   We are the scoffer's creed;
We are the Lord's last message
   Given in deed and word—
What if the line is crooked?
   What if the type is blurred?

What if our hands are busy
   With other work than His?
What if our feet are walking
   Where sin's allurement is?
What if our tongues are speaking
   Of things His lips would spurn?
How can we hope to help Him
   Unless from Him we learn?[1]

—Annie Johnson Flint

Hymn: "O Master, Let Me Walk with Thee" (stanzas 1, 2), or "Make Me a Channel of Blessing" (stanzas 1, 3)

Scripture:

"What doth the Lord thy God require of thee, but to fear the Lord thy God, to walk in all his ways, and to love him, and to serve the Lord thy God with all thy heart and with all thy soul?" (Deuteronomy 10:12). "Now therefore fear the Lord, and serve him in sincerity and in truth" (Joshua 24:14).

Solo: "Satisfied with Jesus" (last half of refrain)

---

1. "Jesus Christ—And We," by Annie Johnson Flint. Copyright. Reprinted by permission, Evangelical Publishers, Toronto 1, Canada.

LEADER:

Is the Master satisfied with my prayers?

> I often say my prayers,
> But do I ever pray;
> And do the wishes of my heart
> Go with the words I say?
>
> I may as well kneel down
> And worship gods of stone,
> As offer to the living God
> A prayer of words alone.
>
> For words without the heart
> The Lord will never hear:
> Nor will he to those lips attend
> Whose prayers are not sincere.

—JOHN BURTON

HYMN: "Did You Think to Pray?" (stanzas 1, 2, 3—refrain after last stanza only)

SCRIPTURE:

"And when thou prayest, thou shalt not be as the hypocrites are: for they love to pray standing in the synagogues and in the corners of the streets, that they may be seen of men. Verily I say unto you, They have their reward. But thou, when thou prayest, enter into thy closet, and when thou hast shut thy door, pray to thy Father which is in secret; and thy Father which seeth in secret shall reward thee openly. But when ye pray, use not vain repetitions, as the heathen do: for they think that they shall be heard for their much speaking. Be not ye therefore like unto them: for your Father knoweth what things ye have need of, before ye ask him. After this manner therefore pray ye" (Matthew 6:5-9).

PRAYER: All pray together the Lord's Prayer.

SOLO: "Satisfied with Jesus" (stanza 4 and refrain)
(Congregation remains with heads bowed during the singing of this final stanza.)

SERVICE 6

THE TOUCH OF THE MASTER'S HAND

SOLO: "Soft Were Your Hands, Dear Jesus"—Geoffrey O'Hara
(Sing first two stanzas of solo here, concluding with "Strong
were your hands, dear Jesus,—Ah, would they had touched
mine.")

POEM:

A Baby's hands in Bethlehem
Were small and softly curled,
But held within their dimpled grasp
The hope of half the world.

A Carpenter's in Nazareth
Were skilled with tool and wood;
They laid the beams of simple homes
And found their labor good.

A Healer's hands in Galilee
Were stretched to all who came
For Him to cleanse their hidden wounds
Or cure the blind and lame.

Long, long ago the hands of Christ
Were nailed upon a tree,
But still their holy touch redeems
The hearts of you and me.[1]

—LESLIE SAVAGE CLARK

SOLO: "Soft Were Your Hands, Dear Jesus"
(Sing last portion of solo here.)

The Touch of the Master's Hand Blesses Little Children

SCRIPTURE READING:

"Then were there brought unto him little children, that he should
put his hands on them, and pray: and the disciples rebuked them.

---

1. "The Hands of Christ," from *Masterpieces of Religious Verse*, edited by James
Dalton Morrison. Copyright, 1948, by Harper & Brothers. Used by permission of the
author.

But Jesus said, Suffer little children, and forbid them not, to come unto me: for of such is the kingdom of heaven. And he laid his hands on them, and departed thence" (Matthew 19:13-15).

HYMN: "I Think When I Read That Sweet Story of Old" (stanza 1)

The Touch of the Master's Hand Heals Broken Bodies

SCRIPTURE READING:

"Now when the sun was setting, all they that had any sick with divers diseases brought them unto him; and he laid his hands on every one of them, and healed them" (Luke 4:40).

HYMN: "At Even, Ere the Sun Was Set" (stanzas 1, 2, 4), or
"The Great Physician" (stanza 1)

The Touch of the Master's Hand Redeems Sin-scarred Souls

POEM:

'Twas battered and scarred and the auctioneer
Thought it scarcely worth his while
To waste much time on the old violin,
But he held it up with a smile.
"What am I bidden, good folk?" he cried.
"Who'll start the bidding for me?
A dollar, a dollar—now two, only two—
Two dollars, and who'll make it three?"
"Three dollars once, three dollars twice,
Going for three"—but no!
From the room far back a gray-haired man
Came forward and picked up the bow;
Then wiping the dust from the old violin,
And tightening up all the strings,
He played a melody pure and sweet,
As sweet as an angel sings.

The music ceased, and the auctioneer,
With a voice that was quiet and low,
Said: "What am I bid for the old violin?"
And he held it up with the bow.
"A thousand dollars—and who'll make it two?
Two thousand—and who'll make it three?
Three thousand once and three thousand twice—
And going and gone!" said he.

The people cheered, but some of them cried,
"We do not quite understand—
What changed its worth?" The man replied:
"The touch of the master's hand!"

And many a man with life out of tune,
And battered and torn with sin,
Is auctioned cheap to a thoughtless crowd,
Much like the old violin.
A "mess of pottage," a glass of wine,
A game—and he travels on,
He's going once, and going twice,
He's going—and almost gone!
But the Master comes, and the foolish crowd
Never can quite understand
The worth of a soul and the change that's wrought
By the touch of the Master's hand.[2]

—MYRA BROOKS WELCH

HYMN: "The Nail-Scarred Hand" (stanzas 1, 4)

*The Touch of the Master's Hand Empowers
Men to Work for Him*

POEM:

My hands were filled with many things
That I did precious hold,
As any treasure of a king's—
Silver, or gems or gold.
The Master came and touched my hands,
(The Scars were in His own)
And at His feet my treasures sweet
Fell shattered, one by one.
"I must have empty hands," said He,
"Wherewith to work my works through thee."

My hands were stained with marks of toil,
Defiled with dust of earth;
And I my work did ofttimes soil,
And render little worth.
The Master came and touched my hands,
(And crimson were His own)
But when, amazed, on mine I gazed,
Lo! every stain was gone.
"I must have cleansed hands," said He,
"Wherewith to work my works through thee."

---

2. From *The Touch of the Master's Hand*, Myra Brooks Welch (Elgin, Illinois: Brethren Publishing House, 1941). Used by permission.

My hands were growing feverish
And cumbered with much care,
Trembling with haste and eagerness,
Nor folded oft in prayer.
The Master came and touched my hands,
(With healing in His own)
And calm and still to do His will
They grew—the fever gone.
"I must have quiet hands," said He,
"Wherewith to work my works through thee."

My hands were strong in fancied strength,
But not in power divine,
And bold to take up tasks at length,
That were not His but mine.
The Master came and touched my hands,
(And might was in His own!)
But mine since then have powerless been,
Save His are laid thereon.
"And it is only thus," said He,
"That I can work my works through thee."

—Author Unknown

HYMN: "Touch Me, Lord Jesus" (stanzas 1, 3), or
"Breathe on Me" (stanzas 3, 4)

The Touch of the Master's Hand Molds Men into His Image

POEM:

Great Master, touch us with Thy skillful hand;
Let not the music that is in us die!
Great Sculptor, hew and polish us; nor let,
Hidden and lost, Thy form within us lie!
Spare not the stroke! do with us what Thou wilt!
Let there be naught unfinished, broken, marred;
Complete Thy purpose that we may become
Thy perfect image,—Thou our God and Lord.

—Horatius Bonar

HYMN: "Have Thine Own Way, Lord" (stanzas 1, 4), or

CHORUS: "Spirit of the Living God, Fall Fresh on Me"

SUGGESTIONS FOR CARRYING OUT THIS SERVICE:

One leader may conduct this entire service, or five different individuals may present each of the five sections which develop the theme.

The poems should be read with deep feeling, and the accompanying hymns sung by the group or by a concealed soloist or quartet.

The latter part of this service can constitute a call to deeper consecration. Use the last hymn as a closing prayer.

SERVICE 7

A MIGHTY FORTRESS IS OUR GOD

HYMN: "O God, Our Help in Ages Past"

RESPONSIVE READING:

Psalm 46. (Leader and group read responsively.)

LEADER:

The truth of these verses is magnificently expressed in a hymn which comes to us out of the long ago—a hymn written by the great "Apostle of the Reformation," Martin Luther. Luther set all Germany to singing the gospel in his hymns of faith, thus teaching the truth of the gospel to the common people, many of whom could neither read nor write. The greatest of these hymns is his "A Mighty Fortress Is Our God," written as a paraphrase on the forty-sixth Psalm, which we have just read responsively. Carlyle said of this hymn: "There is something in it like the sound of Alpine avalanches or the first murmur of earthquakes: in the very vastness of which dissonance a higher unison is revealed to us."

As this hymn has been sung by countless thousands of Christians the world around over a period of four hundred years, its appeal of dauntless courage has never dimmed. Perhaps this is because the writer of its words was one of the most courageous "Soldiers of the Cross" which this world has ever known. "Conflict with 'the prince of darkness grim,' difficulties like a 'flood of mortal ills,' 'the world with devils filled,' 'threatening to undo us'—all of these are reminders of Luther's heroic words on entering the city of Worms in 1521: 'Though there be as many devils in Worms as tiles on the housetops, I must go'; and of the equally heroic declaration before the great Council there: 'I am bound by the Scripture; my conscience is submissive to the will of God. I can recant nothing and will recant nothing.' Triumphantly rings out his confidence in 'the man of God's own choosing,' 'from age to age the same,' who surely 'must win the battle.' "[1]

As we sing this great hymn, let us sing it with triumphant spirit, remembering the dauntless faith of those invincible martyrs of the past who sang it joyfully as they faced persecution and death for the sake of Christ's cause.

HYMN: "A Mighty Fortress Is Our God" (stanza 1)

SCRIPTURE READING:

"The Lord is my light and my salvation; whom shall I fear? the Lord is the strength of my life; of whom shall I be afraid? . . . Though an host should encamp against me, my heart shall not fear: though war should rise against me, in this will I be confident" (Psalm 27:1, 3).

"I can do all things through Christ which strengtheneth me" (Philippians 4:13).

HYMN: "A Mighty Fortress Is Our God" (stanza 2)

SCRIPTURE READING:

"For we wrestle not against flesh and blood, but against principalities, against powers, against the rulers of the darkness of this world, against spiritual wickedness in high places. Wherefore take unto you the whole armour of God, that ye may be able to withstand in the evil day, and having done all, to stand" (Ephesians 6:12-13).

"For whatsoever is born of God overcometh the world: and this is the victory that overcometh the world, even our faith. Who is he that overcometh the world, but he that believeth that Jesus is the Son of God?" (1 John 5:4-5).

"Now thanks be unto God, which always causeth us to triumph in Christ" (2 Corinthians 2:14).

---

1. From *Lyric Religion,* by H. Augustine Smith. Copyright, 1931, Fleming H. Revell Company. Used by permission of the author.

HYMN: "A Mighty Fortress Is Our God" (stanza 3)

SCRIPTURE READING:

"Ye are of God, little children, and have overcome them: because greater is he that is in you, than he that is in the world" (1 John 4:4).

"And the world passeth away, and the lust thereof: but he that doeth the will of God abideth for ever" (1 John 2:17).

HYMN: "A Mighty Fortress Is Our God" (stanza 4)

PRAYER: Of thanksgiving for God's leadership and power as they have been manifested in the past.

LEADER:

Even as this hymn gave fresh courage to the Christians of the long ago, so today it comes with its majestic message of courageous faith, to serve an age that seeks renewed faith in the God who is sufficient for our present need. To Christians of this day comes its challenge to live courageously and victoriously in the faith that this "God of our fathers" is still our "refuge and strength, a very present help in trouble."

POEM:

By the light of burning heretics Christ's bleeding feet I track,
Toiling up new Calvaries ever with the cross that turns not back,
And these mounts of anguish number how each generation learned
One new word of that grand *Credo* which in prophet-hearts hath burned
Since the first man stood God-conquered with his face to heaven upturned.

Careless seems the great Avenger; history's pages but record
One death-grapple in the darkness 'twixt old systems and the Word;
Truth forever on the scaffold, Wrong forever on the throne,—
Yet that scaffold sways the future, and, behind the dim unknown,
Standeth God within the shadow, keeping watch above his own.

—JAMES RUSSELL LOWELL

HYMN: "God of Our Fathers, Whose Almighty Hand"

PRAYER: For courage to do the difficult task, with faith that our God is able to meet our present need as he met the needs of those who lived and died for him in ages past.

SERVICE 8

A SINGING LIFE

MUSICAL MEDITATION: "Living for Jesus"

CALL TO WORSHIP:

"O come, let us sing unto the Lord: let us make a joyful noise to the rock of our salvation. Let us come before his presence with thanksgiving, and make a joyful noise unto him with psalms" (Psalm 95:1-2).

HYMN: "Come, Thou Fount of Every Blessing" (stanza 1)

POEM:

How many of us ever stop to think
Of music as a wondrous magic link
With God; taking sometimes the place of prayer,
When words have failed us 'neath the weight of care?
Music, that knows no country, race or creed;
But gives to each according to his need.

—ANONYMOUS

LEADER:

Music has been called a "language of worship." The earliest sacred music on record is that of the Hebrews, who produced the greatest sacred poet the world has ever known, that "sweet singer of Israel," David. In his hymns of praise, comprising much of Psalms, we hear this melody repeated again and again, "*Come,* let us *sing* unto the Lord." That same call comes to us today—"*Let us sing* unto the Lord; let us make a joyful noise to the rock of our salvation."

And yet someone may say, "I am not musical; I have no great musical gifts; how can I 'sing unto the Lord?' "

Paul, in 1 Corinthians 14:15, says, "I will sing with the *spirit*," and in Ephesians 5:19, he speaks of "making melody in your *heart* to the Lord." And so, even though many of us do not possess beautiful voices with which to sing God's praise, we *can* sing with our lives. A singing life has no need of notes or of musical ability.

> Life gives to every man
> A staff, and a scale of notes.
> The song he sings
> Is one of his own fashioning.
> The world will stop to hear, if it be sweet.
> If it be brave, they will follow him,
> If it be a dirge, they will run away.
>
> Life gives to every man
> A staff, and a scale of notes.[1]
>
> —ALMA LEGGETT LONSDALE

Is the song of your fashioning to be found in these words?

> I would be true, for there are those who trust me;
> I would be pure, for there are those who care;
> I would be strong, for there is much to suffer;
> I would be brave, for there is much to dare.

HYMN: "I Would Be True"

LEADER:

It is not so difficult to sing a song of beauty and of courage when life's pathway is smooth, when loved ones travel by our side, and when the future horizon appears bright and challenging. But the real test of a singing life comes when we must tread the dark valleys alone, when the rays of the sun are hidden, and when even the light of the Son of God is dimmed because of tear-dimmed eyes. But our God "giveth songs in the night," and it is possible to make a song even out of our sorrow, our disappointment, our pain.

> Out of my sorrow I shall make a song
> So beautiful that others' grief will cease.
> If one but listen, silently and long,
> I promise him my song shall bring him peace:
> One clear high note of faith, one note of cheer,
> And one of courage, flung against the sky;
> But not one tremulous, low note of fear,
> And not one muted, agonizing cry.

---

1. "The Score," by Alma Leggett Lonsdale. Used by permission of the author and the *Kansas City Star.*

Oh, I shall make my song a thing of light.
The darkness only can put forth a star;
And out of sorrow—darker than the night—
A song shall lift that men will hear afar,
And listening, with faces, eager—glad—
Will say: "Where is the sorrow that we had?"[2]

—GRACE NOLL CROWELL

HYMN: "Wonderful, Wonderful Jesus" (stanzas 1, 2)

LEADER:

No singing life can be rich and beautiful in its harmonies without the touch of the Master Musician. He awakens the slumbering chords of compassion and tenderness and love; he creates and brings into full fruition the capacities which are ours for beauty and strength and Christlike living. For our "Fairest Lord Jesus" even "makes the woeful heart to sing."

HYMN: "Fairest Lord Jesus" (stanza 2)

LEADER:

"O come, let us sing unto the Lord"; let us make "melody in our *hearts* to the Lord!"

Lord—I would have my sweetest song to be
A life attuned to perfect harmony,
No minor chords to add a deeper grief
To hearts already finding much to weep.

No! rather let my life of beauty sing;
Of sparkling happiness like songs of spring,
And now and then let come a quiet strain
To comfort some poor, lonely heart in pain.

Let every word and deed when heard alone
Give forth the richness of some perfect tone;
Together, make a symphony of chords,
A harmony to please my Lord of Lords!

ZULA E. COON

HYMN: "I'll Live for Him," or
"Now in the Days of Youth" (See Service 1)

---

2. "A Song from Sorrow," from *Songs for Courage* by Grace Noll Crowell (New York; Harper and Brothers, 1938). Used by permission.

SERVICE 9

"GOD GIVE ME MOUNTAINS"

MUSICAL MEDITATION: "This Is My Father's World," or
                   "For the Beauty of the Earth"
CALL TO WORSHIP:

> God give me mountains
> With hills at their knees,
> Mountains too high
> For the flutter of trees,
>
> Mountains that know
> The dark valleys of death,
> That have kissed a pale star
> And felt its last breath
>
> And still lift the dawn
> In a golden-rimmed cup—
> God give me mountains,
> And strength to climb up![1]

—LEIGH HANES

("Mountains," by Oscar Rasbach, in solo or SATB arrangement, may be used instead of the poem if desired. Words identical.)

LEADER:

Mountains! How beautifully God speaks of them in his written Word; how many times he chooses a mountain upon which to reveal himself, or to teach some precious truth to our needy hearts and lives! As did the psalmist of old, let us "lift up our eyes unto the hills" and see what lessons they have to teach us.

SOLO OR CHOIR: "I Will Lift Up Mine Eyes"—F. Flaxington Harker, or

---

1. "Mountains," by Leigh Hanes. Used by permission of the author.

SOLO: "I Will Lift Up Mine Eyes"—Alfred Wooler, or
"On a Hill" (a spiritual)—Lola Gibson Deaton
(This latter song relates the many incidents which took place "on a hill" in the Bible narrative.)

LEADER:

"God give me mountains"—that they may teach me to be strong and steadfast in faith and in courage.

1ST READER:

"They that trust in the Lord shall be as mount Zion, which cannot be removed, but abideth for ever. As the mountains are round about Jerusalem, so the Lord is round about his people from henceforth even for ever. . . . For the Lord is a great God, and a great King above all gods. . . . The strength of the hills is his also" (Psalms 125:1-2; 95:3-4).

2ND READER:

> The fairest flowers these eyes have seen,
>   With fullest fragrance and in colors rare,
> Are those which drink the sweetness of the peaks,
>   And flourish in the sunshine and the mountain air!
>
> And can it be, my soul, that life grows strong,
>   That beauty deeper and more lasting crowns our day,
> As we, with tired feet but hearts undaunted,
>   Still onward push, and upward, on our way?
>
> What matters if the heights be hard to gain?
>   What matter if the road shall narrow be?
> With every turn the vision fairer grows.
>   Lord, let me walk the mountain peaks with Thee![2]
>
> —RALPH SPAULDING CUSHMAN

HYMN: "Higher Ground" (stanzas 1, 2)

LEADER:

"God give me mountains"—that they may teach me the ways of quietness and of peace.

---

2. "The Heights," from *Hilltop Verses and Prayers,* by Ralph Spaulding Cushman. Copyright, 1945, by Whitmore & Stone. By permission of Abingdon-Cokesbury Press.

1ST READER:

"The mountains shall bring peace to the people, and the little hills, by righteousness" (Psalm 72:3).

2ND READER:

How often Jesus realized the truth of this promise as he went "into a mountain apart":

> Whenever the Master could, He stole away
> From the great throngs to seek some quiet place
> Where He could be alone, where He could pray,
> Where God could come to meet Him face to face.
> Strange strength is ever born of solitude;
> The heart today grows weary of its care
> And over-burdened . . . God, it would be good
> To seek a mountain side and find Thee there.
>
> Christ stole away at evening to the hills.
> So should we go, the press of the day's work done,
> To seek some quiet place where the last light spills
> The radiant splendor of the setting sun,
> And kneel to pray. How often we have lost
> The way to solitude, and at such cost![3]
>
> —GRACE NOLL CROWELL

SOLO: "Christ Went Up into the Hills"—Richard Hageman, or

HYMN: "Still, Still with Thee" (stanzas 1, 2)

LEADER:

"God give me mountains"—that they may teach me vision, and then lead me from the mountaintop of vision into the valley of service.

1ST READER:

"And after six days Jesus taketh Peter, James, and John his brother, and bringeth them up into a high mountain apart, and was transfigured before them: and his face did shine as the sun, and his raiment was white as the light. And, behold, there appeared unto them Moses and Elias talking with him. Then answered Peter, and said unto Jesus, Lord, it is good for us to be here: if thou

---

3. "Into a Mountain Apart," from *Songs of Hope* by Grace Noll Crowell (New York; Harper and Brothers, 1938). Used by permission.

wilt, let us make here three tabernacles; one for thee, and one for
Moses, and one for Elias. While he yet spake, behold, a bright
cloud overshadowed them: and behold a voice out of the cloud,
which said, This is my beloved Son, in whom I am well pleased;
hear ye him. And when the disciples heard it, they fell on their
face, and were sore afraid. And Jesus came and touched them,
and said, Arise, and be not afraid. And when they had lifted up
their eyes, they saw no man, save Jesus only. . . . And it came to
pass, that on the next day, when they were come down from the
hill, much people met him" (Matthew 17:1-8; Luke 9:37).

2ND READER:

> Stay, Master, stay upon this heavenly hill;
> A little longer, let us linger still;
> With all the mighty ones of old beside,
> Near to God's holy presence still abide;
> Before the throne of light we trembling stand,
> And catch a glimpse into the spirit-land.
>
> Stay, Master, stay! we breathe a purer air;
> This life is not the life that waits us there:
> Thoughts, feelings, flashes, glimpses come and go;
> We cannot speak them—nay, we do not know;
> Wrapt in this cloud of light we seem to be
> The thing we fain would grow—eternally.
>
> "No!" saith the Lord, "the hour is past," we go;
> Our home, our life, our duties lie below.
> While here we kneel upon the mount of prayer,
> The plow lies waiting in the furrow there!
> Here we sought God that we might know his will;
> There we must do it, serve him, seek him still.
>
> If man aspires to reach the throne of God,
> O'er the dull plains of earth must lie the road:
> He who best does his lowly duty here,
> Shall mount the highest in a nobler sphere:
> At God's own feet our spirits seek their rest,
> And he is nearest him who serves him best.

—SAMUEL GREG

HYMN: "Where Cross the Crowded Ways of Life" (stanzas 1, 2, 4,
       5)

LEADER:

"God give me mountains"—that they may teach me to worship and to praise until the "King of glory" comes.

1ST READER:

"For ye shall go out with joy, and be led forth with peace: the mountains and the hills shall break forth before you into singing, and all the trees of the field shall clap their hands" (Isaiah 55:12).

2ND READER:

They stand, the regal mountains, with crowns of spotless snow,
Forever changeless, grand, sublime, while ages come and go!
Each day the morning cometh in through the eastern gate,
With trailing robes of pink and gold; yet still they watch and wait
For that more glorious morning, till that glad message sounds—
"Lift up your hearts, ye gates of God! the King of glory comes!"

And so they stand o'erlooking earth's trouble, pain and sin,
And wait the call to lift their gates and let the King come in.
O calm, majestic mountains! O everlasting hills!
Beside your patient watch how small seem all life's joys and ills!

—ANONYMOUS

HYMN: "Praise Him! Praise Him!" (stanza 3), or
ANTHEM: "Lift Up Your Heads" (See Appendix II for arrangements.)

SERVICE 10

"THE LORD IS MY SHEPHERD"

(Service based on the twenty-third Psalm)

MUSICAL MEDITATION: "He Shall Feed His Flock" from *The Messiah*—Handel

SOLO: "The Good Shepherd"—Van de Water, or

SOLO OR CHOIR: "The Twenty-third Psalm"—Malotte, or

HYMN: "The Lord Is My Shepherd"
> (If the other stanzas of the hymn are being used later in the service, use only the first stanza here.)

1ST READER: *"The Lord is my Shepherd."*

2ND READER: What more could heart desire for Life's long journey
> Than just to claim this promise of His care
> For every weary mile that must be traveled,
> For sun-kissed days when all the world is fair?
> He is the Way, the Truth, the Life Eternal
> To little lambs, to older sheep as well,
> Who, weak or strong, depend upon His guidance
> To keep them from the path where danger dwells.

HYMN: "Saviour, Like a Shepherd Lead Us" (stanzas 1, 2)

1ST READER: *"I shall not want."*

2ND READER: Here is a promise greater than all others,
> A Shepherd's promise to the one He loves:
> "I shall not want,"—for food, for strength, for comfort;

He sends His gifts abundant from above.
"I shall not want" if all the way He leadeth
With sorrow or with singing be supplied,
He satisfies the needs of soul and spirit,
What more could any follower ask beside?

HYMN: "All the Way My Saviour Leads Me" (stanzas 1, 2)

1ST READER: *"He maketh me to lie down in green pastures."*

2ND READER: The Shepherd knows the way to pleasant meadows,
He guides the weary, worn and wandering feet
Of every sheep and lamb till rest is realized
In some green pasture strangely cool and sweet;
And there He binds their wounds while they are
resting,
He bids them rest till they are tired no more,
Then, all refreshed and ready for life's journey,
They go once more, their Shepherd on before.

HYMN: "Near to the Heart of God" (stanza 1), or
"I Heard the Voice of Jesus Say" (stanza 1), or

SOLO OR CHOIR: "Green Pastures"—Sanderson

1ST READER: *"He leadeth me beside the still waters."*

2ND READER: The Shepherd knows not only rest is needed
For weary feet which travel Life's rough road,
But there is need for *quiet* and for *stillness*—
"Be still and know"—this is His spoken Word.
He speaks to those who anxious are and troubled,
He bids them turn from ways of feverish will
To quiet paths, where, after storm and tempest,
His still, small voice can whisper, "Peace, be still."

HYMN: "Jesus, Saviour, Pilot Me" (stanza 2), or
"Dear Lord and Father of Mankind" (stanzas 1, 3, 4), or

SOLO OR CHOIR: "Beside Still Waters"—Hamblen

1ST READER: *"He restoreth my soul; He leadeth me in the paths of righteousness for his name's sake."*

2ND READER: The Psalmist knew that each must bear some burden,
He cried, "Why art thou cast down, O my soul?"
He knew the miracle of restoration
As floods of living water o'er him rolled.
With confidence restored, with courage heightened,
He sang once more in faith, "He leadeth me,"
Knowing the Shepherd's paths are to be trusted,
Tho' they may lead by still or troubled sea.

HYMN: "He Leadeth Me" (stanzas 1, 2)

1ST READER: *"Yea, though I walk through the valley of the shadow of death, I will fear no evil: for thou art with me; thy rod and thy staff they comfort me."*

2ND READER: The Shepherd's love and care are *fully* realized
When He must lead into the valley deep,
Full well He knows were Life all pleasant meadows,
No growth would come to His beloved sheep.
He knows their need for what the valley teaches,
So, tenderly, with heed to every cry,
He draws them close beside Him in the darkness,
And leadeth them where deepest shadows lie.

HYMN: "The Lord Is My Shepherd" (stanza 2), or

SOLO OR CHOIR: "Trust in Him"—Hamblen

1ST READER: *"Thou preparest a table before me in the presence of mine enemies: thou anointest my head with oil; my cup runneth over."*

2ND READER: There is no word of praise that one can utter
That fully tells the Shepherd's gracious gifts,
His table is prepared in love and mercy,
His cup o'erflows when pressed to thirsty lips,
His followers find His goodness multiplying

Each joyful mile they travel by His side,
And His companionship grows far more precious
The more they in His loving arms abide.

HYMN: "The Lord Is My Shepherd" (stanza 3), or
"Praise Him! Praise Him! (stanza 1)

1ST READER: *"Surely goodness and mercy shall follow me all the days of my life: and I will dwell in the house of the Lord for ever"* (Psalm 23).

2ND READER: The Shepherd trail has led through pleasant meadows,
By waters still and over troubled sea,
The paths of righteousness, the shadowed valley,
Are all within the way "He leadeth me"—
No path too difficult, no trail too lonely,
Until at last, beyond the journey's end,
The Shepherd opens wide the heavenly sheepfold,
And greets His sheep as their eternal Friend!

ZULA E. COON

HYMN: "The Lord Is My Shepherd" (stanza 4), or

SOLO, DUET OR CHOIR: "The King of Love My Shepherd Is"—
Shelley

SUGGESTIONS FOR CARRYING OUT THIS SERVICE:

It is suggested that two readers be used for this service, one for the Scripture passages, and one for the accompanying stanzas of poetry. This service could be presented by a choir, the choir and soloists from the choir singing the hymns, anthems, and solos suggested. Several selections have been suggested in some instances so that the service may be adapted to a simple or a more elaborate presentation.

SERVICE 11

"I WILL MAKE YOU"

MUSICAL MEDITATION: "Where He Leads Me"

SCRIPTURE:

"Jesus said unto them, Come ye after me, and *I will make you* to become fishers of men" (Mark 1:17).

HYMN: "Jesus Calls Us" (stanza 1)
(Sung by concealed soloist)

LEADER:

One day, as Jesus walked by the sea of Galilee, he called to some fishermen as they cast their nets into the sea, saying, "Come ye after me, and *I will make you*,"—and Simon the unstable, the impetuous, the weak, became Peter the rock, the leader of the twelve, upon whose great confession Christ's church has been built.

> Peter cast his nets in the blue of Galilee;
> Peter reaped the harvests of the wave-fields of the sea;
> He caught the silver fishes for the food of every day . . .
> Or he told tall tales of those who got away.
>
> Bold and brusque was Peter; his heart and speech were free
> As the fierce waves running down the length of Galilee;
> His rough hair red as a sun-browned reed,
> And his gray eyes glinting with the daring and the deed.
>
> Peter knew the peril and perversity of wind;
> Peter knew the anger of the great waves dinned;
> Deep he felt the urging and the utter need that drives
> Men to make a living to the forfeit of their lives.
>
> Peter knew the black boats, with bilge about his feet;
> Peter drew the black nets where panic fishes beat;
> The midnight was lonely and the sea was full of graves
> And the fog like ghostly thickets growing palely from the waves.

Peter in the dawn was weary with the night;
Peter saw the black fish grow silver in the light;
Eagerly he dropped the net and fumbled for the oar—
Now for food and now for sleep upon the firmer shore!

Peter from the little boat sees someone on the sand;
Peter the untamable obeys a strange command;
Who is this that glimmers like a Sun beyond the sun?—
"Behold, the voyage is over—and the voyage is begun!"

Peter hears the voice that can bid the storm be still;
Peter the willful obeys a mightier will;
His life has been a barren sea made monstrous with the night;
But now the sun is risen and the mists dissolve in light.

"You have been a fisher—and you shall fish again:
For come, and *I will make you* a Fisherman of Men."
Peter goes to voyage upon a vaster sea;
Peter goes to cast his nets into Eternity.[1]

—E. MERRILL ROOT

HYMN: "Jesus Calls Us" (stanza 4)
(Sung by concealed soloist)

LEADER:

Jesus also called to two other fishermen that day, saying, "Come ye after me, and *I will make you*,"—and the two sons of Zebedee, the "sons of thunder," became James and John of the "inner circle," —disciples, apostles, witnesses of the Christ who taught them to fish for men.

It was enthusiasm that led James and John, at the call of Christ, to fling down their nets and forsake their boats and there and then, without thought of the future, leave all to become the followers of One "who had not where to lay his head." In keeping with this intense enthusiasm and sacrificial decision, "James came one day with his brother John, when, though they did not know it, only seven more days stood between Jesus and His bitter cross, and already his face was 'set toward Jerusalem'—they came at that time with their ungenerous ambitions and self-centered request: 'Grant that we may sit, one on thy right hand and one on thy left hand, in thy glory' (Mark 10:35-41).

---

1. "Fisher of Men," from *Before the Swallow Dares*, by E. Merrill Root. Copyright, 1947, by Packard & Co., Chicago, publishers. Used by permission of the author.

"The answer of Jesus to that ambitious petition was free from all harshness. He knew that they did not understand, and with that Infinite patience which always characterized His dealings with them He proceeded to explain the situation. They desired to be at His side at the Great Banquet; He put to them the question therefore: 'Are ye able to drink the cup that I drink?'

"Jesus knew these two men better than the disciples knew them—better even than they knew themselves. He knew that they were capable of higher ambitions than these which so greatly angered their brethren. As they answered His question with the words: 'We are able,' He foresaw that they would indeed share His cup of sacrificial pain, and drink it giving glory to God for so high a fellowship of suffering, and therefore He dealt tenderly though seriously with them. But He has left us in no doubt concerning the way to sovereignty: we must climb 'the steep ascent of heaven, through peril, toil and pain'; the greatest in the kingdom are the servants of all."[2]

HYMN: "Are Ye Able?" (stanza 1)
    (Sung by concealed soloist)

LEADER:

Jesus called one day to a woman bound in the prison-house of sin, and Mary of Magdala, the slave to sin, became Mary Magdalene, the pure, the devoted, the first herald of the Master's triumph over the grave. Hear her as she tells her own story:

> I was a slave to Sin—
> My fevered soul imprisoned in the dark—
> Possessed of seven devils, I became
> Despised and outcast from the ways of men.
>
> And then *He* came—
> He looked into my heart, all touched with flame,
> He looked into my soul, all seared with sin,
> He looked into my 'mind, so small with self's desire,
> And in that look I caught a glimpse of Love's infinitude.

---

2. From *The Inner Circle,* by Trevor H. Davies, D.D. Copyright, 1924, George H. Doran Company.

I looked,—and saw One lovely as a rose,
I looked,—and saw One pure as sun-kissed snow,
I looked,—and all my selfish sin and shame
Fell like an old gray cloak at Jesus' feet.

My heart is now aflame with living fire,
My soul is now grown tall with selfless love,
My mind now reaches high to meet the mind of God,
And in His Light I walk the trail with God.

I am a slave to Love—
But oh, this Love is broad and deep and high,
Its compass is not bound by narrow ways
Of self and sin and pleasure's hour,
But rather is it boundless as God's love,
Which in its wonder reaches down to those
Who tread the paths of sin's dark night,
And lifts and lights into a Son-blessed day
Where Christ, the Son of God, is glorified.

His Love now overflows my sin-cleansed soul,
His Peace is deep and fathomless within,
His chastening fires have purified and made me whole,
Till Love's pure fire now burns alone for Him.

ZULA E. COON

HYMN: "O Love That Wilt Not Let Me Go" (stanzas 1, 4), or
"Jesus Paid It All" (stanzas 1, 2, 3)
(Sung by concealed soloist)

LEADER:

One day, as Jesus passed by the receipt of custom, he called to
a despised taxgatherer, and Levi the publican became Matthew the
flaming evangel, the recorder of the King. There was no rest for
Matthew until he answered this call; only then were his feet led
into the paths of peace. He speaks to us therefore across the years
as one who knows the truth of what he tells:

> Long did I toil, and knew no earthly rest,
> Far did I rove, and found no certain home;
> At last I sought them in His sheltering breast,
> Who opes His arms, and bids the weary come:
> With Him I found a home, a rest divine,
> And I since then am His, and He is mine.

The good I have is from His stores supplied,
The ill is only what He deems the best;
He for my Friend, I'm rich with nought beside,
And poor without Him, though of all possessed:
Changes may come—I take, or I resign,
Content, while I am His, while He is mine.

—JOHN QUARLES and HENRY F. LYTE

HYMN: "I Heard the Voice of Jesus Say" (stanza 1)
      (Sung by concealed soloist)

LEADER:

Throughout all the years which have passed since Jesus called to men and women of his day, saying, "Come ye after me, and *I will make you*," his voice has sounded down the corridors of time to Christians of every land and every age, pleading that they leave all and follow him. We may not always understand his will and way; we may not always choose to follow; but if and when we do respond to his persistent pleading, we find that he will "make us," too—transforming the unstable, unpromising character traits of newborn Christians into the steadfastness and devotedness of these of the long ago, whose transformation was wrought by the miracle touch of the Man of Galilee.

To each of us Jesus is calling today, saying, "Come ye after me, and *I will make you*." Are *you* willing to let him "make you" what he *can* and *will?* May we bow our heads and search our hearts, and if you are willing to let him "make you," you will want to sing with us as we sing very softly our pledge of dedication.

HYMN: "Where He Leads Me" (stanza 1 and refrain), or
      "Footsteps of Jesus" (stanza 1 and refrain)

PRAYER OF CONSECRATION

SERVICE 12

THE VICTORY OF DEFEAT

MUSICAL MEDITATION: "The Son of God Goes Forth to War"

LEADER:

On the lips of many in the past few years have been heard the words "victory" and "defeat." But these words refer to the victory and defeat of men and of nations; only in God's Word can that paradox be found which we might call "The Victory of Defeat!"

I sing the hymn of the conquered, who fell in the Battle of Life,—
The hymn of the wounded, the beaten, who died overwhelmed in the strife;
Not the jubilant song of the victors, for whom the resounding acclaim
Of nations was lifted in chorus, whose brows wore the chaplet of fame,
But the hymn of the low and the humble, the weary, the broken in heart,
Who strove and who failed, acting bravely a silent and desperate part;
Whose youth bore no flower in its branches, whose hopes burned in ashes away,
From whose hands slipped the prize they had grasped at, who stood at the dying of day
With the wreck of their life all around them, unpitied, unheeded, alone,
With Death swooping down o'er their failure, and all but their faith overthrown,
While the voice of the world shouts its chorus,—its paean for those who have won;
While the trumpet is sounding triumphant, and high to the breeze and the sun
Glad banners are waving, hands clapping, and hurrying feet
Thronging after the laurel-crowned victors, I stand on the field of defeat,
In the shadow, with those who are fallen, and wounded, and dying, and there
Chant a requiem low, place my hand on their pain-knotted brows, breathe a prayer,
Hold the hand that is helpless, and whisper, "They only the victory win,
Who have fought the good fight, and have vanquished the demon that tempts us within;
Who have held to their faith unseduced by the prize that the world holds on high;
Who have dared for a high cause to suffer, resist, fight—if need be, to die.

Speak, History! Who are Life's victors? Unroll thy long annals and say;
Are they those whom the world called the victors, who won the success of a
    day?
The martyrs, or Nero? The Spartans, who fell at Thermopylae's tryst,
Or the Persians and Xerxes? His judges, or Socrates, Pilate or Christ?

                               —WILLIAM W. STORY

HYMN: "The Son of God Goes Forth to War" (stanza 1)

LEADER:

The Son of God goes forth to war? How—on a cross of shame?
Without weapons? Defenseless against infuriated enemies? Yes! !
For this strange paradox of the "Victory of Defeat" is exemplified
in no greater way than on that hill far away where stood an "old
rugged cross" on which our Saviour died for the sins of the world.

If ever there was a triumph over seemingly the most disastrous
defeat in history, it was the triumph of the cross. We see him
standing in Pilate's hall, not conquering by his replies to the ac-
cusations of his enemies, nor by the use of physical force, but
rather by the quality of his spirit and by his complete silence. We
see him hanging on a cross of shame, and in that apparent defeat
bringing to the world the greatest triumph it has ever known—a
triumph which offers redemption to the whole wide world.

HYMN: "The Old Rugged Cross" (stanzas 1, 3), or
              "When I Survey the Wondrous Cross" (stanzas 1, 3)

LEADER:

Let us now think of that great conquering host of men and women
who have followed in the train of this victorious Son of God.
They are the ones who would not be defeated, who would not compromise or yield to overwhelming obstacles, but who have gone on
and on, with heads erect, hearts brave, defying defeat and disaster.
With few exceptions, those who come down to us on history's pages
as the truly great have been thwarted and hindered and defeated
all along the pathway of life.

We remember that out of the defeat of the first Christian martyr,
Stephen, came a victory which paved the way for a worldwide conquest for Christ.

Hymn: "The Son of God Goes Forth to War" (stanza 2)

Leader:

Out of the defeat of twelve valiant disciples of the Christ, who "met the tyrant's brandished steel" and "mocked the cross and flame," came a victory which passed the torch to all valiant "soldiers of the cross" throughout the ages to come.

Hymn: "The Son of God Goes Forth to War" (stanza 3)

Leader:

Out of the defeat of Paul in a Roman prison cell came the victory which sent the gospel even down to our world today.

Out of the defeat of a dying missionary in a simple hut in central Africa came the victory which resulted in the redemption of the Dark Continent.

We could name many, many more—that "noble army" who "climbed the steep ascent to heaven, thro' peril, toil, and pain," whose mastery over difficulties gave to them the victory which can come only through the Lord Jesus Christ.

Hymn: "The Son of God Goes Forth to War" (stanza 4)

Leader:

Can *we* live this overcoming life? We do not feel that we are made of the stuff of which heroes are made. Is it possible for us to know this "Victory of Defeat?" Many of us have known times of complete bewilderment, of despair, of defeat. Can *we* conquer, too? What is the secret of this conquering power?

Christ taught men to conquer by using his own weapon—perfect love that casteth out fear—and not the weapons of the world. A practical application of such love is implied in his own words: "Put up thy sword" (John 18:11); "Love your enemies, bless them that curse you, do good to them that hate you, and pray for them which despitefully use you, and persecute you" (Matthew 5:44). Our banner will be the blood-stained banner of the crucified Christ, our sword will be the Word of God, and our victory will be a victory of love and not of hate. "Love cannot be defeated, . . . for a life of love is deathless, even in death, and victorious even in defeat."[1]

HYMN: "Lead On, O King Eternal" (all stanzas)

LEADER:

There is something bigger in man than circumstances or sorrow or the power of evil; there is something finer than human eye can see. That something within us is the presence and power of the triumphant Christ which makes possible even for *us* the "Victory of Defeat" over temptation, sorrow, misfortune, fear—*anything!* "Ye are of God, little children, and have overcome them: because *greater is he that is in you,* than he that is in the world" (1 John 4:4).

Sorrows come, dreams are broken, plans are shattered, hope gone, but the victory which Christ gives is greater than all these, for through the gateway of defeat we pass into a richer, fuller and more victorious life. Yes, we, too, can conquer, "Thanks be unto God, which always causeth us to triumph in Christ" (2 Corinthians 2:14).

HYMN: "Fight the Good Fight," or
      "Forward Through the Ages," or
      "A Mighty Fortress Is Our God"

---

1. From *The Christ of the Mount,* by E. Stanley Jones. Copyright, 1931, by the Abingdon Press. Used by permission.

Section II

The few services in this section have been planned for longer periods of time when an entire worship service is given over to a service in song. In them, the selection of the number of stanzas to be used has been left to the worship leader, except when only one or two of the stanzas, rather than the entire hymn, have fitted the thought preceding the hymn. In the latter cases, these stanzas have been suggested.

SERVICE 13

THE CHRISTIAN TRAIL

INTRODUCTION

Today we are going on a journey, down a trail which every one of us who names the name of Christ must travel. It is the trail of the Christian life, beginning in the *morning* of life, continuing through its *noonday*, and culminating in the *sunset* hour when we shall see our Master "face to face."

But before we begin to travel this trail, I want each of you to go with me down another trail—a trail of the long ago, and picture a scene enacted there. It is late afternoon, and on a road leading down to a swift-running river stand three young men, intently absorbed in conversation. Our attention is especially drawn to the one who appears to be the accepted leader of the three, for he is a man who would attract attention anywhere. It is not his clothing which attracts, for it is coarse and plain, even to the point of severeness. Neither are we impressed by the handsomeness of his face, for it is in reality spare and thin, suggesting a diet as severely plain as his garments. No, rather is it the earnestness, the intentness of his countenance which holds our gaze, for his eyes glow like coals of fire under thick, bushy eyebrows; and as he talks, we feel that the passion of his life lies in his quiet, intense words.

As we look at the two to whom he is speaking, we note that they are sharply contrasted in appearance, yet both are equally intent on what their leader is saying. In the face of the one there is a fineness and a depth of feeling, almost ascetic in quality; the other is more the sort of fellow one would meet in the market place or on the busy thoroughfare—a practical, matter-of-fact looking individual who quietly listens and has little to say.

As they talk, a fourth man, a Stranger, comes down the road, passes the three companions and goes on down the trail leading to a village near by. Quickly the leader speaks a word to his two companions, and even more quickly they leave his side to follow the trail which the Stranger is traveling. It is not long before the Stranger turns to the two who are following in his footsteps and asks them the simple question, "Whom are you looking for?" Taken aback and hardly knowing what to answer, they timidly ask the Stranger where he is going, to which he graciously replies, "Come, and you shall see." The two men gladly accept the invitation, and then and there a friendship is born which lasts through the lives of all three of these young men—and, yes, even throughout eternity!

Perhaps you have already recognized the young men of our story. First, John the herald, the leader of the three, who, during his conversation with his two followers, John and Andrew, looked down the road and saw Jesus coming toward them. And, the important point of our story is this: *"Looking unto Jesus as he walked, he said, Look!"* John and Andrew's contact with Jesus began in *looking.*

THE MORNING OF LIFE

The Call

And so it is with all of us who begin to travel the trail with Jesus in the *morning* of life. The invitation, "Come, and you shall see," may come to each of us in a different way. Some herald of the King may say to us, "Look!"—and, looking, we begin to travel the trail of the Son of God. Or it may be in some quiet place alone as he speaks to us through his Book, or through the still, small voice, that we hear his gracious invitation, "Come, and make my paths your choice."

HYMN: "Come, Says Jesus' Sacred Voice" (stanzas 1, 4)

The Acceptance

And so, let us picture ourselves as having heard this call of "Follow me," as having accepted its challenge, and in full acceptance of that challenge, our faith *looks up to Him,* and we pray:

> Take all my guilt away,
> Oh, let me from this day
> Be wholly Thine.

HYMN: "My Faith Looks Up to Thee"

The Privilege of Prayer

Now let us look once more at the picture of that friendship formed between the three young men of the long ago. John and Andrew went from their first *looking* unto Jesus into closer contact. First, they *looked* at Jesus; then they *talked* with him. We do not know just how long that first talk lasted—perhaps two hours, perhaps longer—but we do know that those two never got over that talk which they had with their new-found Friend that twilight hour. From that hour, they got into the habit of referring everything to him; of bringing problems and needs and even joys to him; and of judging everything by what he had to say.

So it is with us—after our first *looking* unto Jesus—we seek to know him better by *talking* with him. And out of those first talks with him grows the habit of talking with him *all* the time— in the thick of the crowd, in the solitude of our homes, in the midst of our work—in every circumstance or condition of life our hearts learn to speak to him. Our common name for it is *prayer*. Often we neglect this priceless privilege; but the more we make use of it, the more we find—"What a Friend we have in Jesus, all our sins and griefs to bear! What a privilege to carry everything to God in prayer!"

HYMN: "What a Friend"

The Companionship of His Word

Not only do we talk with him in this new-found relationship, but we also find him talking with us, for we have the companionship of his Word.

In a very lovely story, Margaret E. Sangster has told of the Bible which was given to her by her grandmother while she was yet a very little girl. Written in the Bible was the expressed wish of her grandmother, "I hope that she will read it and love it all of her life!" And in reply to this hope, Margaret Sangster has written: "Oh, friends of mine, I have done just that. I have gone to my Bible when trouble walked beside me, and the path was too dark for me to travel without the comfort of a guiding light. I have come to my Bible when my heart was singing—singing 'Glory to God in the Highest,' and 'Alleluia, Alleluia.' I have come to it heavily laden—and have found rest. I have sought it when I was torn with doubt and I have found the peace that passes understanding. I have come to it poor in spirit and body—and have always found something to enrich me. I have gone to it lacking in faith and have felt faith flow warmly back into my heart."[1]

This is the gift which her grandmother gave to her in the morning of life. Christ has an even greater gift for each of us in the *morning* of life—a companionship with him as he breaks to us the "bread of life" through his Word.

HYMN: "Break Thou the Bread of Life," or "Holy Bible, Book Divine"

Living for Jesus

Once more we learn from our story out of the long ago. These two young men went from their talking *with* Jesus to talking with others *about* him. Their personal contact with him was the beginning of their service. You recall how each went to his own family first—Andrew finding his brother, Peter; John, his brother, James. And so we, too, find that the next step in our new relationship with Jesus is that we desire above all else to tell others *about* him. "Living for Jesus" becomes the compelling desire of our lives.

HYMN: "Living for Jesus," or
     "I Love to Tell the Story"

THE NOONDAY OF LIFE

All-Out For Christ

And now we pass into the *noonday* of life. Things which appeared bright and beautiful in the *morning* of life may not look as

---

1. From "My First Bible," *Christian Herald*, October, 1937. Used by permission of the author.

promising now. The glare of the noonday sun wearies our courageous spirits and blinds the vision that made the way so clear in the
morning of life. Not always now do we hear the still, small Voice,
for other voices are calling for us to turn this way or that, and we
find that unless we keep very close to our unseen Companion of
the Way, we could easily go astray. He may even call us into a
path which we would not choose for ourselves, and we face a
struggle within until we have yielded our will completely unto
his will. 'Tis then we pray:

Laid on Thine altar, O my Lord Divine,
    Accept my will this day, for Jesus' sake;
I have no jewels to adorn Thy shrine—
    Nor any world-proud sacrifice to make;
But here I bring within my trembling hand,
    This will of mine—a thing that seemeth small,
And Thou alone, O God, canst understand
    How, when I yield Thee this, I yield mine all.

Hidden therein, Thy searching gaze can see
    Struggles of passion—visions of delight—
All that I love, and am, and fain would be,
    Deep loves, fond hopes, and longings infinite.
It hath been wet with tears and dimmed with sighs,
    Clinched in my grasp, till beauty hath it none—
Now, from Thy footstool where it vanquished lies,
    The prayer ascendeth, "May Thy will be done."

Take it, O Father, ere my courage fail,
    And merge it so in Thine own Will, that e'en
If, in some desperate hour, my cries prevail,
    And Thou give back my will, it may have been
So changed, so purified, so fair have grown,
    So one with Thee, so filled with peace divine,
I may not see nor know it as my own,
    But, gaining back my will, may find it Thine.

—MORNE WALLIS

With this victory won, there comes a complete dedication of our
all to the Master, and we can say as never before, "Take my life
and let it be consecrated, Lord, to Thee." (Change wording if
another hymn is used.)

HYMN: "Take My Life, and Let It Be," or
"I Surrender All," or
"My Jesus, As Thou Wilt"

Service as Soldiers of the Cross

There are also battles to fight for our Master in the *noonday* of life; therefore, we must "put on the whole armour of God, that ye may be able to stand against the wiles of the devil. For we wrestle not against flesh and blood, but against principalities, against powers, against the rulers of the darkness of this world, against spiritual wickedness in high places. Wherefore take unto you the whole armour of God, that ye may be able to withstand in the evil day, and having done all, to stand. Stand therefore, having your loins girt about with truth, and having on the breastplate of righteousness; and your feet shod with the preparation of the gospel of peace; above all, taking the shield of faith, wherewith ye shall be able to quench all the fiery darts of the wicked. And take the helmet of salvation, and the sword of the Spirit, which is the word of God: Praying always with all prayer and supplication in the spirit" (Ephesians 6:11-18).

HYMN: "Am I a Soldier of the Cross?"

His Keeping Power

If we have kept very close to our Master in the *noonday* of life; if we have surrendered our wills and lives to him and proved ourselves worthy "soldiers of the cross," then we shall realize and rejoice in his marvelous *keeping power*—in the "firm foundation" which we have laid for ourselves in Christ Jesus, our Lord.
HYMN: "How Firm a Foundation"

THE SUNSET OF LIFE

Now we come at last to the *sunset* of life, and turn to look backward over the years which have made up the *morning* and the *noonday* of our lives.

Yet who, thus looking backward o'er his years,
Feels not his eyelids wet with grateful tears,
                If he hath been
Permitted, weak and sinful as he was,
To cheer and aid, in some ennobling cause,
                His fellow-men?

If he hath hidden the outcast, or let in
A ray of sunshine to the cell of sin,—
                If he hath lent
Strength to the weak, and, in an hour of need,
Over the suffering, mindless of his creed
                Or home, hath bent,

He has not lived in vain, and while he gives
The praise to Him, in whom he moves and lives,
                With thankful heart;
He gazes backward, and with hope before,
Knowing that from his works he nevermore
                Can henceforth part.

—JOHN G. WHITTIER

Thus we can say with Paul, that great "soldier of the cross," "For I am now ready to be offered, and the time of my departure is at hand. I have fought a good fight, I have finished my course, I have kept the faith: henceforth there is laid up for me a crown of righteousness, which the Lord, the righteous judge, shall give me at that day: and not to me only, but unto all them also that love his appearing" (2 Timothy 4:6-8).

Assurance and Praise

For the faithful Christian, these sunset days are filled with a blessed assurance and a song of praise. No doubt or fear can now overtake us, for we are persuaded "that neither death, nor life, nor angels, nor principalities, nor powers, nor things present, nor things to come, nor height, nor depth, nor any other creature, shall be able to separate us from the love of God, which is in Christ Jesus our Lord" (Romans 8:38-39).

HYMN: "Blessed Assurance"

Trail's End

And now—the end of the Trail!

POEM: "Crossing the Bar"

> (This may be sung as a solo or quartet, or read as a closing
> poem while quiet music is played.)

Sunset and evening star,
And one clear call for me!
And may there be no moaning of the bar,
When I put out to sea,

But such a tide as moving seems asleep,
Too full for sound and foam,
When that which drew from out the boundless deep
Turns again home.

Twilight and evening bell,
And after that the dark!
And may there be no sadness of farewell
When I embark;

For tho' from out our bourne of Time and Place
The flood may bear me far,
I hope to see my Pilot face to face
When I have crossed the bar.

—ALFRED TENNYSON

SUGGESTIONS FOR CARRYING OUT THIS SERVICE:

One leader may direct this service, or each section (Introduction,
Morning of Life, Noonday of Life, Sunset of Life) may be led
by a different individual. The hymns should be sung by the entire
congregation. Have the outline of the service, together with the
hymns to be used with each section, placed on a blackboard before
the group or mimeographed and given out to each individual.

NOTE:—The stories of John and Andrew in this service are adapted from S. D.
Gordon's book, *Quiet Talks on Service*, published by Fleming H. Revell Co. Used by
permission.

SERVICE 14

"WHEN IS THE TIME FOR PRAYER?"

HYMN: "The Beautiful Garden of Prayer"

CALL TO WORSHIP:

"Evening, and morning, and at noon, will I pray, and cry aloud: and he shall hear my voice" (Psalm 55:17).

> When is the time for prayer?
> In every hour, while life is spared to thee—
> In crowds or solitude—in joy or care—
> Thy thoughts should heavenward flee.
> At home—at morn and eve—with loved ones there,
> Bend thou the knee in prayer!
>
> —ANONYMOUS

PRAYER: That Christ will lead us daily into the "beautiful garden of prayer" and there teach us to pray.

LEADER:

A young Christian, seeking to grow in his new life with Christ, might well ask the question, "*When* is the time for prayer?" In seeking to answer this question, we here present a typical day in the life of a Christian, and the place which prayer should have in that day in order to give added strength and power and beauty to the life of the one who prays. As we sing and pray together, may all of us be led to pray, not only at some stated time during the day, but to "pray without ceasing," that the events of every day, whether large or small, may be brought under the touch of his power—because we have prayed.

Someone has beautifully described prayer as "the Key of the Day and the Lock of the Night." Every day comes to us with its own peculiar burdens, its own problems, its own needs, and calls us to prayer of various kinds. The early morning hour brings a challenge for the day; the glare of the noonday sun finds us in the battle of life with all its struggles and cares; finally, the day's end comes with its welcome quiet and rest after the toil of the day, and each of these presents a special need for prayer.

READER:

> When is the time for prayer?
> With the first beams that light the morning sky,
> Ere for the toils of day thou dost prepare,
> Lift up thy thoughts on high;
> Commend thy loved ones to his watchful care:
> *Morn is the time for prayer!*

—ANONYMOUS

(Music of "Whisper a Prayer" played as the following poem is read.)

> A moment in the morning, ere the cares of the day begin,
> Ere the heart's wide door is open for the world to enter in,
> Ah, then, alone with Jesus, in the silence of the morn,
> In heavenly sweet communion, let your duty-day be born.
> In the quietude that blesses with a prelude of repose
> Let your soul be smoothed and softened, as the dew revives the rose.
>
> . . . .
>
> A moment in the morning—a moment, if no more—
> Is better than an hour when the trying day is o'er.
> 'Tis the gentle dew from heaven, the manna for the day;
> If you fail to gather early—alas! it melts away.
> So, in the blush of morning, take the offered hand of love,
> And walk in heaven's pathway and the peacefulness thereof.

—ARTHUR LEWIS TUBBS

SOLO OR QUARTET: "Whisper a Prayer" (stanza 1)

LEADER:

For what shall we pray as we "whisper a prayer in the morning?" Christ taught us *first* to pray, "Thy kingdom come. Thy will be done in earth, as it is in heaven." So, in the early morning hour, our prayer must encompass the needs of the whole wide world.

PRAYER HYMN: "O God, We Pray for All Mankind"
(For words of this hymn, see Service 34)

LEADER:

We shall also need to bring our own personal needs to the feet of the Master as we "whisper a prayer" in the early morning hour.

Dear Lord, who sought at dawn of day the solitary woods to pray,
In quietness we come to seek Thy guidance for the coming day.
O Master, who with kindly face at noon walked in the market place,
We crave a brother's smile and song, when mingling in the human throng.
Strong Pilot, who at midnight hour could calm the sea with gentle power,
Grant us the skill to aid the bark of those who drift in storm and dark.
As Thou at weary eventide communed upon the mountain-side,
In reverent stillness now we ask Thy presence in the daily task.

—W. L. CURRY

PRAYER HYMN: "Lord, for Tomorrow and Its Need," or
                    "Just for Today"

LEADER:

Ruskin said, "If you do not wish for His Kingdom, don't pray for it. But if you do, you must do more than pray for it, you must work for it." Having committed the peoples of all lands as well as our own personal needs to the Master in the early morning hour, we are now ready to go out to work for Christ's kingdom, equipped with his power, his strength, his very living presence.

PRAYER:

"Unto Thee, O Lord, do I lift up mine eyes, Thou who dwellest in the heavens. Help me this day to make of earth a little bit of Heaven, to make a sanctuary unto Thee in all the common places where I walk, to find Thee every hour a living Presence near, to help my comrades of the day to find Thee too. So may Thy will be done in me this day. In Christ's dear Name. Amen."[1]

(Continue the prayer period with the singing of one stanza of the hymn, "Sweet Hour of Prayer")

---

1. From *Hilltop Verses and Prayers,* by Ralph Spaulding Cushman. Copyright, 1945 by Whitmore & Stone. By permission of Abingdon-Cokesbury Press.

LEADER:

We now enter into the tasks, the struggles, the problems of the day. Here is where we must meet temptation; here is where we may even face defeat. Not only is there need for prayer in the morning and in the evening hour; if ever prayer is needed, it will be needed in the glare of the noonday sun.

READER:

> And in the noontide hour,
> If worn by toil and by sad care oppressed,
> Then unto God thy spirit's sorrows pour,
>   And he will give thee rest:
> Thy voice shall reach him through the fields of air:
>   *Noon is the time for prayer!*

—ANONYMOUS

(Music of "Whisper a Prayer" played as the following poem is read)

> "For evening and morning are not enough;
> The day is long, and the road is rough;
> As the heat increases, strong men grow weak;
> New strength from above your soul must seek."
>
> And that's how I learned at the noon of the day
> To lift mine eyes and steal away,
> At least in thought, to some quiet place,
> Where I sit with the Master face to face![2]

—RALPH SPAULDING CUSHMAN

SOLO OR QUARTET: "Whisper a Prayer" (stanza 2)

LEADER:

Jesus said, "Watch and pray, that ye enter not into temptation: the spirit indeed is willing, but the flesh is weak" (Matthew 26:41). He also taught us to pray, "Lead us not into temptation, but deliver us from evil" (Matthew 6:13). Many times during the day there may be need for this prayer, for temptation may beset us upon every hand. However, we have the assurance that in the hour

---

2. From poem, "Evening and Morning and Noon Will I Pray." From *Spiritual Hilltops*, by Ralph S. Cushman. Copyright, 1932, by Ralph S. Cushman. By permission of Abingdon-Cokesbury Press.

of trial Jesus will plead for us, even as he pleaded for Simon Peter in his hour of trial. You will remember the words of the Lord Jesus when he said, "Simon, Simon, behold, Satan hath desired to have you, that he may sift you as wheat: but *I have prayed for thee,* that thy faith fail not" (Luke 22:31-32).

PRAYER HYMN: "In the Hour of Trial"

LEADER:

During the day, we must not forget to pause for a prayer of thanksgiving.

> I am so grateful. Lord, today,
> I must kneel down to pray,
> To thank Thee, not alone for bread,
> And for my sheltering roof, my bed,
> But for a thousand splendid things
> My glad heart lifts and sings.
>
> For eyes to see the sun's good light;
> For ears to hear the swift-winged bright
> Voice of the birds, and the wind through trees,
> The fragrances upon the breeze,
> The velvet touch of leaf and flower;
> Thy care about me, hour by hour,
> Thy hand, unseen, that guides me through
> The day's length with its work to do,
> And gently, tenderly the while
> Down every straight and crooked mile,
> Thy *Word,* its promises that glow
> To guide me as I go.
> I am so grateful, Lord, for these,
> I thank Thee now upon my knees.[3]
>
>   —GRACE NOLL CROWELL

HYMN: "For the Beauty of the Earth," or
       "When Morning Gilds the Skies"

LEADER:

Again, our prayer throughout the day would not be Christlike in its pattern if we failed to make the burden of our prayer for *others.*

----

3. Used by permission of the author.

For how many loved ones and friends and even acquaintances can we say during the day, "For you I am praying?" As we sing this prayer-hymn, may we make this a time of silent intercessory prayer for those who most need our prayers just now.

PRAYER HYMN: "I Am Praying for You"

(After the first stanza has been sung, the pianist may continue playing the hymn softly through a period of silent prayer; then modulate to the hymn, "Softly Now the Light of Day.")

SOLO OR QUARTET: "Softly Now the Light of Day"

READER:

> When the bright sun hath set,
> Whilst yet eve's glowing colors deck the skies,
> When with the loved, at home, again thou'st met,
>   Then let thy prayers arise
> For those who in thy joys and sorrows share:
>   *Eve is the hour for prayer!*

—ANONYMOUS

(Music of "Whisper a Prayer" played as the following poem is read.)

> The shadows of the evening hours
> Fall from the darkening sky;
> Upon the fragrance of the flowers
> The dews of evening lie:
> Before Thy throne, O Lord of heaven,
> We kneel at close of day;
> Look on Thy children from on high,
> And hear us while we pray.
>
> . . . .
>
> Let peace, O Lord, Thy peace, O God,
> Upon our souls descend;
> From midnight fears and perils, Thou
> Our trembling hearts defend.
> Give us a respite from our toil,
> Calm and subdue our woes;
> Through the long day we labor, Lord,
> O give us now repose.

—ADELAIDE A. PROCTER

SOLO OR QUARTET: "Whisper a Prayer" (stanza 3)

LEADER:

As we whisper a prayer at the twilight, the events of the day pass slowly through our minds. This is the time when we bring the failures, the mistakes, the heartaches of the day to our Heavenly Father, and ask for forgiveness, for cleansing and for healing.

SOLO: "An Evening Prayer"

READER:

> And when the stars come forth—
> When to the trusting heart sweet hopes are given
> And the deep stillness of the hour gives birth
> To pure bright dreams of heaven—
> Kneel to thy God; ask strength life's ills to bear:
> *Night is the time for prayer.*
>
> —ANONYMOUS

BENEDICTION HYMN: "Now the Day Is Over"

SUGGESTIONS FOR CARRYING OUT THIS SERVICE:

Have the group participate in the singing of as many of the prayer hymns as possible. The others may be sung by a soloist or a quartet. The three stanzas of "Whisper a Prayer" introduce the three periods of prayer, beginning (1) "Whisper a prayer in the morning," (2) "Whisper a prayer at the noontime," (3) "Whisper a prayer at the twilight."

Have printed programs with names of hymns and prayers so that these can be participated in without announcement. Sing each prayer hymn as a prayer, with bowed heads.

SERVICE 15

MOSAICS OF THE MASTER

SOLO: "We Would See Jesus" (stanzas 1, 4)

LEADER:

In the days of the long ago, when Jesus lived and walked among men, certain Greeks came to one of his disciples one day saying, "*Sir, we would see Jesus.*" Today, in our bewildered, sin-ridden world, there are countless troubled souls looking to those of us who are his present-day disciples and saying, "We, too, would see Jesus!" How are they to see him today, this invisible Christ, if not through us who have already seen him and known him through the eyes of the spirit? Well can we remember when we caught our first vision of him in his beauty! The world was then touched with a new beauty; life took on a richer meaning; and a peace that was beyond our understanding took the place of our restless longings and fears. And now there are others, all around us, who stand restless and fearful, and say to us, "Disciples who name the name of Christ, *we would see Jesus—in you!*" In this pathetic plea each professing Christian finds his own special call to service, and each must seek his own way of meeting the crucial challenge; and, in meeting it, each will have his own part in the creation of a *mosaic of the Master!*

We are told that a mosaic is one of the rarest and most beautiful of all the works of art. It is made by putting together thousands of tiny pieces of marble or glass of many colors so as to make pictures or patterns. The colors blended in some of these works of art comprise as many as 28,000 different shades! In Rome there is a mosaic of Peter which took ten men nine years to construct.

As we find new beauties in the Christ day by day and seek to portray those beauties in our own lives, let us ever remember that we are making a mosaic of Christ, placing the precious stones, blending the beautiful colors, so that this work becomes *our* master-piece, *our* work of art. If it took ten men nine years to make such a picture of Peter, surely it will take us a lifetime to construct a mosaic of Christ, and even when we pass into eternity and see him "face to face," we shall doubtless find that much of the beauty and wonder to be found in him has been omitted from our earthly work.

Let us consider a few of the stones which shall go into our mosaic of Christ.

The first precious stones which we shall place in our mosaic are the blood-red stones of sacrifice and the scarlet stones of love— "*God so loved . . . that he gave. . . .*" When we first survey the wondrous cross on which our Saviour died, all other sights dim before our eyes, and we see only the vivid red of his nail-torn hands and feet, and the scarlet wound of his pierced side.

Solo: "Why Should He Love Me So?"

Leader:

These vivid red stones set in our mosaic as we view his cross are only the beginning of the scarlet motif, for the more we come to know our Master and the more his love is manifested to us in countless precious ways, the more we realize that the predominant color in our pattern *must* be the scarlet hue of love and of sacrifice.

Hymn: "Love Divine, All Love Excelling"

Leader:

As our lives grow "in wisdom and in stature" as followers of the Christ, we add still more stones to our masterpiece. We look at his life and see that he "went about doing good"; we marvel at his compassion and tenderness toward every individual who crossed his pathway; and, slowly, instinctively, our own hearts warm to the needs of those about us; our own hands go out in loving kindness to meet those needs, and we find that we have added the royal purple to our work of art—purple stones of compassion and of kindness.

Hymn: "O Master, Let Me Walk with Thee," or
  "O Brother Man, Fold to Thy Heart Thy Brother"

Leader:

But these vivid hues of purple and of red are not enough. They must be tempered and softened by softer tones to make the master-piece a thing of balance and of beauty. One does not look long at the character of Christ without recognizing that here we find the shining radiance of perfect purity—purity of heart and life, purity of thought and purpose, purity that sees God even while in the flesh. You will remember that it was Christ himself who said, "Blessed are the pure in heart, for they shall see God." Because his heart was pure, he lived constantly in the presence of his Heavenly Father, seeing him while he lived among men. His followers who place the shining white stones of purity in their mosaic will also catch a glimpse of the glories of their Father-God.

Hymn: "Purer in Heart, O God"

Leader:

Another softer tone to be blended with the more vivid hues is the rose-gray stone of peace. When we first place our hand in the nail-scarred Hand, this peace steals into our hearts quietly, and we experience a deeper peace than we have ever known before—the Master's peace—lovelier than the rose-gray line of sunset, softer than the rose-gray velvet of a dove's warm wing, more tender than the rose-gray loveliness of an old-fashioned mother—"sweet peace, the gift of God's love."

Hymn: "Sweet Peace, the Gift of God's Love"

Leader:

Not only do we find perfect purity and perfect peace in the character of Christ, but also we marvel at the picture of his in-comparable faith. You will remember that he faced and conquered his tempter in the wilderness with the shield of faith and the sword of the Spirit; you will recall how he "set his face toward Jerusalem" with faith in the ultimate outcome; finally, in the end, he faced Gethsemane and Golgotha with a faith that triumphed on an Easter morning. He constantly admonished his followers to "have faith in God"; he taught them that all things are possible to those who have sufficient faith in his promises; he sought faith in others and marveled when he found great faith in those who sought his help.

Many stones of faith must be placed in our mosaic of the Master, and what color could be more fitting to portray such faith than that of the fresh, new green of the springtime—the green of grass and tree and flower which comes forth each spring to give us promise of the resurrection. And so the stones of faith become a part of our masterpiece, and we marvel more and more at the beauty of the Subject whose picture we are painting in precious stones.

HYMN: "My Faith Looks Up to Thee," or
        "O, For a Faith That Will Not Shrink," or
        "Have Faith in God"

LEADER:

One color still is lacking. No work of art would be complete without the azure blue of the heavens, and so we add the blue of humility. Where could greater humility be found than that which we see in Christ Jesus, "who, being in the form of God, thought it not robbery to be equal with God: but made himself of no reputation, and took upon him the form of a servant, and was made in the likeness of men: and being found in fashion as a man, he humbled himself, and became obedient unto death, even the death of the cross" (Philippians 2:6-8).

Perhaps the azure blue stone of humility is the most difficult one of all for us to fit into our mosaic. There is so much pride within our nature; there is so much desire for self-exaltation and self-praise, that we sometimes forget that One long ago spoke these words to his followers: "He that is greatest among you shall be your servant. And whosoever shall exalt himself shall be abased;

and he that shall humble himself shall be exalted" (Matthew 23:
11-12).

HYMN: "When I Survey the Wondrous Cross" (stanzas 1, 2)

LEADER:

As we have placed each stone in its proper place, we have come
to understand far more about the love and sacrifice of Christ, about
his kindness and compassion, his purity and his peace, his faith and
his humility. But still our knowledge of him is incomplete. Some
of the most beautiful bits of the mosaic cannot be fashioned until
we ourselves have tasted of the sufferings of the Master, until we
have gone down into the "valley of the shadow" with him alone,
until we have borne our own smaller Gethsemanes and Calvaries.

"That I may know him, and the power of his resurrection, and
the *fellowship of his sufferings*," says Paul. And as we enter into
this fellowship with him—the fellowship of his sufferings—the scarlet hues of his love become more vivid, the rose-gray tints of his
peace fall more softly over our needy hearts, the purple of his
compassion deepens into richer shades, the emerald of his faith
kindles the waning confidence of our own hearts, and our mosaic
takes on a beauty and a richness of coloring unknown before. And
to the mosaic is now added the golden glow of patience. For "the
trying of your faith worketh patience. But let patience have her
perfect work, that ye may be perfect and entire, wanting nothing"
(James 1:3-4).

HYMN: "Are Ye Able?" or
       "Jesus, I My Cross Have Taken"

LEADER:

Surely it will take a lifetime for us to complete our masterpiece,
and still there will be beauties undreamed of when we reach the
other side. "For now we see through a glass, darkly; but then face
to face: now I know in part; but then shall I know even as also
I am known" (1 Corinthians 13:12).

HYMN: "Face to Face"

LEADER:

The most wonderful thing about the making of our mosaic of Christ is that, as we seek to know him and to be like him, the work of art becomes *a part of us,* and we unconsciously show forth to the world the likeness of the One whose image we are fashioning.

As we gaze into the face of Christ, as we come to know him personally, our own personalities are merged and gradually lost in his greater personality, and our mosaic becomes in reality *Christ living in us!*

Because we see in him supreme love, we, too, learn to love our neighbor as ourselves; because we find in him perfect purity, our own thoughts and actions are purified; because he "went about doing good," this becomes the supreme passion of our lives; because his peace has comforted us in times of distress, we seek to bring comfort into other lives; because he taught us to have faith, our faith becomes like that of a little child; because he walked the paths of earth as a humble servant of man, we, too, are humbled into selfless service; because he suffered victoriously, our suffering becomes a blessed fellowship rather than a senseless suffering.

However, one word of caution may be needful; for indifference, neglect, selfishness, sin, and many other things may mar our work and leave it unfinished and unlovely. If this be true, the world will fail to see the image of Christ through our lives; but if we give *our best* to our mosaic-making, others, too, will catch the vision, and our mosaic will have accomplished its purpose in helping to lead the world to the feet of the Master.

May we bow our heads and very quietly and very reverently sing as our closing prayer, "Let the Beauty of Jesus." (Change wording if another hymn is used.)

CHORUS: "Let the Beauty of Jesus," or

HYMN: "Jesus Revealed in Me," or
"More Like the Master"

SERVICE 16

WINDOWS OF THE SOUL

MUSICAL MEDITATION: "Breathe on Me," or
"Take Time to Be Holy"

CALL TO WORSHIP:

"I will hew great windows, wonderful windows, measureless windows for my soul."[1]

POEM:

Let there be many windows in your soul,
That all the glory of the universe
May beautify it. Not the narrow pane
Of one poor creed can catch the radiant rays
That shine from countless sources. Tear away
The blinds of superstition. Let the light
Pour through fair windows, broad as truth itself,
And high as heaven . . . Tune your ear
To all the wordless music of the stars,
And to the voice of Nature; and your heart
Shall turn to truth and goodness as the plant
Turns to the sun. A thousand unseen hands
Reach down to help you to their peace-crowned heights;
And all the forces of the firmament
Shall fortify your strength. Be not afraid
To thrust aside half-truths and grasp the whole.[2]

—ELLA WHEELER WILCOX

LEADER: *I will hew a window of Love,*

For, lo! in hidden deep accord
The servant may be like his Lord.
And Thy love, our love shining through,
May tell the world that Thou art true,
Till those who see us see Thee too.

—ANNA LETITIA WARING

---

1. From "Room," by Angela Morgan. Permission granted by the author.

2. "Windows of the Soul," from *Poems of Progress*, by Ella Wheeler Wilcox, Copyright, 1909, W. B. Conkey Company. Used by permission of the publishers.

HYMN: "More Love to Thee"

LEADER: *I will hew a window of Joy, for*

It is a comely fashion to be glad;
Joy is the grace we say to God.

—JEAN INGELOW

HYMN: "Joyful, Joyful, We Adore Thee"

LEADER: *I will hew a window of Peace, for*

I need wide spaces in my heart,
Where faith and I can go apart
  And grow serene.
Life gets so choked by busy living,
Kindness so lost in fussy giving,
  That Love slips by unseen.

—AUTHOR UNKNOWN

HYMN: "Dear Lord and Father of Mankind" (last two stanzas)

LEADER: *I will hew a window of Longsuffering, for*

Well to suffer is divine.
Pass the watchword down the line,
  Pass the countersign, Endure!
Not to him who rashly dares,
But to him who nobly bears,
  Is the victor's garland sure.

—JOHN G. WHITTIER

HYMN: "Am I a Soldier of the Cross?"

LEADER: *I will hew a window of Gentleness and Kindness, for*

The Holy Supper is kept, indeed,
In whatso we share with another's need;
Not what we give, but what we share,
For the gift without the giver is bare;
Who gives himself with his alms feeds three—
Himself, his hungering neighbor, and Me.

—JAMES RUSSELL LOWELL

HYMN: "O Brother Man, Fold to Thy Heart Thy Brother," or
"Master, No Offering Costly and Sweet"

LEADER: *I will hew a window of Goodness, for*

"The serene, silent beauty of a holy life is the most powerful influence in the world, next to the might of God."—
Pascal

HYMN: "My Prayer," or
"Take Time to Be Holy"

LEADER: *I will hew a window of Faith, for*

Faith is the grasping of Almighty power;
The hand of man laid on the arm of God;
The grand and blessed hour
In which the things impossible to me
Become the possible, O Lord, through Thee.

—ANNA E. HAMILTON

HYMN: "O For a Faith That Will Not Shrink"

LEADER: *I will hew a window of Meekness and Humility, for*

Thy home is with the humble, Lord!
  The simplest are the best,
Thy lodging is in child-like hearts;
  Thou makest there Thy rest.

Dear Comforter! Eternal Love!
  If Thou wilt stay with me,
Of lowly thoughts and simple ways
  I'll build a house for Thee.

—FREDERICK W. FABER

HYMN: "Pass Me Not, O Gentle Saviour," or
"How Beauteous Were the Marks Divine"

LEADER: *I will hew a window of Temperance and Self-Control.*

White Captain of my soul, lead on;
I follow Thee, come dark or dawn.
Only vouchsafe three things I crave:
Where terror stalks, help me be brave!
Where righteous ones can scarce endure
The siren call, help me be pure!
Where vows grow dim, and men dare do
What once they scorned, help me be true![3]

—ROBERT FREEMAN

HYMN: "Dare to Be Brave, Dare to Be True," or
"My Soul, Be on Thy Guard"

LEADER:

We now see that Paul's "fruit of the Spirit" may become the windows of our soul—love, joy, peace, longsuffering, gentleness, goodness, faith, meekness, temperance (Galatians 5:22-23).

Let us pray silently that the Spirit of the living God may build within the temple of our souls these great and wonderful windows for his glory.

DIRECTED PRAYER:

(To be read as a prayer while pianist plays softly, "Breathe on Me." During the pauses for silent prayer, the music continues.)

O master Carpenter of life, help us to hew many windows for our souls that the light of the Lord Jesus may shine through us to light a world in darkness.

(Pause for silent prayer.)

Open a window wide to thy love that we may learn to love thee supremely and others unselfishly.

(Pause for silent prayer.)

May thy joy shine forth from our lives from springs deep down within, and may its source be the One "who for the joy that was set before him endured the cross, despising the shame, and is set down at the right hand of the throne of God" (Hebrews 12:2).

---

3. Used by permission of Mrs. Robert Freeman.

(Pause for silent prayer.)

Give to us the blessing of thy peace that it may dwell in our inmost spirits to give serenity and calm in the midst of the fret and fever of life.

(Pause for silent prayer.)

Let patience have her perfect work within us that we may be perfect and entire, wanting nothing.

(Pause for silent prayer.)

Create within us a gentle and a compassionate spirit that we may "follow with reverent steps the great example of Him whose holy work was 'doing good.' "

(Pause for silent prayer.)

"Let Thy goodness, like a fetter, bind our wandering souls to Thee" until the window of our souls may reflect only thy holiness and thy love.

(Pause for silent prayer.)

Enlarge the window of our faith until we shall believe steadfastly in the God of the impossible and prove faithful in helping him to do the impossible in and through us.

(Pause for silent prayer.)

O meek and lowly Nazarene, carve a window of humility out of our proud and wilful hearts that we may be servants of all, even of those lowlier than ourselves.

(Pause for silent prayer.)

Give to us, Master of the mastered life, a mastery of self which will lead us forth as victors in life's conquest until the final conquest leads us unto thee.

(Pause for silent prayer.)

This we ask in the spirit and in the name of Christ. Amen.

SUGGESTIONS FOR CARRYING OUT THIS SERVICE:

An effective use of this service would be for a quartet or choir to sing the hymns suggested, and for different individual members of quartet or choir to give the readings, "I will hew a window of. . . ." The service may be used also with one leader and congregational singing of the hymns.

SECTION III

In this section, the worship leader will find two or three worship services built around each subject. The intended use for such services is that the two or three programs on each subject be used in consecutive services; i.e., consecutive Sundays, consecutive noon-day prayer services, conference themes, etc., in order that the theme may be developed in its entirety through a series of programs. The time for each of these services is approximately fifteen minutes or less.

SERVICE 17

I LOVE THY CHURCH, O GOD

The Personal Ministry of the Church

CALL TO WORSHIP (quartet or choir): "O Church of God" (Tune: "Finlandia")

O Church of God, our solitude forsaking,
We now unite with all who seek thy way—
With those who sing, with those whose hearts are breaking,
We lift our spirits as to God we pray;
O Church of God, our love for thee is waking,
We bring our alleluias today.

O Church of God, like bells at noon-day pealing,
Thy call has come to us that we may bring
Our strength to serve, to all the Christ revealing
In deeds of love and when our hopes take wing;
O Church of God, where sin and pain find healing,
To thee our alleluias we sing.

Our Spirit's Home, with joy to thee returning,
Our voices join to sing our highest praise,
For hours of cheer, where friendship's fires are burning,
For strength and peace which gladden all our days;
O Church of God, for thee our hearts are yearning,
To thee our alleluias we raise.[1]

—ROLLAND W. SCHLOERB

---

1. Used by permission of the author.

POEM:

> Thou, whose unmeasured temple stands,
> Built over earth and sea,
> Accept the walls that human hands
> Have raised, O God, to Thee.
>
> And let the Comforter and Friend,
> Thy Holy Spirit, meet
> With those who here in worship bend
> Before Thy mercy seat.
>
> May they who err be guided here
> To find the better way;
> And they who mourn, and they who fear,
> Be strengthened as they pray.
>
> May faith grow dim, and love grow warm,
> And pure devotion rise,
> While round these hallowed walls the storm
> Of earth-born passion dies.
>
> —WILLIAM CULLEN BRYANT

HYMN: "I Love Thy Kingdom, Lord" (stanzas 1, 2)

1ST READER:

"I Love Thy Church, O God" because it is a house of worship.

2ND READER:

"O come, let us worship and bow down: let us kneel before the Lord our Maker. For he is our God; and we are the people of his pasture, and the sheep of his hand. . . . Honour and majesty are before him: strength and beauty are in his sanctuary. . . . O worship the Lord in the beauty of holiness" (Psalms 95:6-7; 96:6, 9).

HYMN: "O Worship the King" (all stanzas), or
 "In Thy Holy Temple" (stanzas 1, 2)

1ST READER:

"I Love Thy Church, O God" because it teaches the Word of God.

2ND READER:

Concerning the early apostles of the New Testament church, it was said, "And daily in the temple, . . . they ceased not to teach and preach Jesus Christ" (Acts 5:42). From that time even down to the present, as his Word has been taught in the house of God, men have realized anew that "the word of God is quick, and power- ful, and sharper than any twoedged sword" (Hebrews 4:12).

HYMN: "O Word of God Incarnate" (stanzas 1, 2), or
       "Wonderful Words of Life" (stanzas 1, 2)

1ST READER:

"I Love Thy Church, O God" because it is a house of prayer.

2ND READER:

"Even them will I bring to my holy mountain, and make them joyful in my house of prayer: . . . for mine house shall be called an house of prayer for all people" (Isaiah 56:7).

HYMN: " 'Tis the Blessed Hour of Prayer" (stanzas 1, 2)

READING: (Copies of the following reading may be placed in the hands of each person present and read in unison, if de- sired.)

"My church is the place where the Word of God is preached, the power of God is felt, the Spirit of God is manifested, the love of God is revealed, and the unity of God is perceived.

"It is the home of my soul, the altar of my devotion, the hearth of my faith, the center of my affections, and the foretaste of heaven.

"I have united with it in solemn covenant, pledging myself to attend its services, to pray for its members, to give to its support, and to obey its laws.

"It claims the first place in my heart, the highest place in my mind, the principal place in my activities, and its unity, peace, and progress concern my life in this world and that which is to come.

"I owe it my zeal, my benevolence, and my prayers. When I neg-lect its services, I injure its good name, I lessen its power, I dis-courage its members, and I chill my own soul.

"I have solemnly promised in the sight of God and men to ad-vance its interests by my faithful attendance, by reading the Holy Bible, by never neglecting its ordinances, by contributing to its support, by meeting with my fellow members, by watching over their welfare, and by joining with them in prayer and praise and service; and that promise I this day renew, before God my Father, Christ my Redeemer, and the Holy Spirit, my Sanctifier."[2]

HYMN: "I Love Thy Kingdom, Lord" (stanzas 2, 3, 4, 5)

PRAYER:

"O God, we pray for thy Church, which is set today amid the perplexities of a changing order, and face to face with a great new task. We remember with love the nurture she gave to our spiritual life in its infancy, the tasks she set for our growing strength, the influence of the devoted hearts she gathers, the steadfast power for good she has exerted. When we compare her with all other human institutions, we rejoice, for there is none like her. But when we judge her by the mind of her Master, we bow in pity and contri-tion. Oh, baptize her afresh in the life-giving spirit of Jesus! . . . Put upon her lips the ancient gospel of her Lord. . . . Fill her with the prophets' scorn of tyranny, and with a Christlike tender-ness for the heavy-laden and down-trodden. . . . Bid her cease from seeking her own life, lest she lose it. Make her valiant to give up her life to humanity, that like her crucified Lord she may mount by the path of the cross to a higher glory. Amen."[3]

---

2. From F. F. Brown's article in *The Baptist Student*, November, 1948.

3. From *Prayers of the Social Awakening*, by Walter Rauschenbusch. The Pilgrim Press. Used by permission.

SERVICE 18

I LOVE THY CHURCH, O GOD

The Ultimate Triumph of the Church

HYMN: "Zion Stands with Hills Surrounded," or
"Glorious Things of Thee Are Spoken"

CALL TO WORSHIP:

O where are kings and empires now
Of old that went and came?
But, Lord, Thy Church is praying yet,
A thousand years the same.

We mark her goodly battlements,
And her foundations strong;
We hear within the solemn voice
Of her unending song.

For not like kingdoms of the world,
Thy holy Church, O God;
Though earthquake shocks are threat'ning her,
And tempests are abroad.

Unshaken as eternal hills,
Immovable she stands,
A mountain that shall fill the earth,
A house not made by hands.

—ARTHUR CLEVELAND COXE

HYMN: "I Love Thy Kingdom, Lord" (stanzas 1, 2)

1ST READER:

"I Love Thy Church, O God" because it is built upon the foundation of Jesus Christ.

2ND READER:

"For other foundation can no man lay than that is laid, which is Jesus Christ" (1 Corinthians 3:11). "Christ also loved the church, and gave himself for it; . . . that he might present it to himself a glorious church, not having spot, or wrinkle, or any such thing; but that it should be holy and without blemish" (Ephesians 5:25, 27).

HYMN: "The Church's One Foundation" (stanza 1)

1ST READER:

"I Love Thy Church, O God" because it has a message of salvation for all the world.

2ND READER:

"The voice of rejoicing and salvation is in the tabernacles of the righteous" (Psalm 118:15). "How beautiful upon the mountains are the feet of him that bringeth good tidings, that publisheth peace; that bringeth good tidings of good, that publisheth salvation; that saith unto Zion, Thy God reigneth!" (Isaiah 52:7).

HYMN: "The Church's One Foundation (stanza 2)

1ST READER:

"I Love Thy Church, O God" because, in spite of trial and persecution, it shall ultimately triumph and become the church victorious.

2ND READER:

For Jesus said, "Upon this rock I will build my church; and the gates of hell shall not prevail against it" (Matthew 16:18).

HYMN: "The Church's One Foundation" (stanza 3)

POEM:

> O Church of God triumphant, above the world's dark fears;
> In thee our souls find refuge through all these earthly years,
> Christ's steadfast holy purpose, illumined by the cross,
> When hosts encamp against us, reveals their might but dross.

Her bells on Christmas morning have set our hearts aglow,
At Easter-time her carols with faith still over-flow;
Within her sacred portals our children learn God's truth,
While at her hallowed altars to Christ we pledge our youth.

Through manhood's sterner challenge, in womanhood's brave years,
The Church of Christ continues in gladness or in tears,
To guide our footsteps onward till sunset's lingering rays
Reveal God's Heavenly Country beyond our earthly days.

O Church of God triumphant, we pledge anew in prayer,
Our youth, our fuller manhood, for Christ's great cause to dare;
Till his redeeming purpose shall prove beyond defeat,
When gather all God's children around His Mercy seat.[1]

—S. RALPH HARLOW

HYMN: "I Love Thy Kingdom, Lord" (stanzas 2, 3, 4, 5)

PRAYER:

"God of the rushing wind and the flaming tongue, we pray for Thy church, . . . so beset with bewilderment in a new and confused time.

"Heal it of ancient schism, we pray thee; purge it of pride, and renew the vision grown dim in its heart.

"Teach us, O Lord, that it is not by might, nor by power, but by Thy spirit, that the Gospel will run and be glorified through us, sending Thy light and Thy truth into the dark places of the earth.

"Spirit of light and power, at whose altar we bow,

"Rekindle a heroic and mighty faith in the heart of Thy Church;

"Let not the gates of hell prevail against it.

"May it be baptized anew with the spirit of unity, the flame of vision, and the sacrificial passion of Christ, that its stammering voice may become a redeeming anthem in a discordant world.

"In the name of Jesus Christ, our Lord. Amen."

"Flames of Fire"—AUTHOR UNKNOWN

PRAYER HYMN (sung softly as a solo while heads remain bowed in prayer): "O Word of God Incarnate" (stanza 4 and Amen)
    (The tune, "Aurelia," to which "The Church's One Foundation" is sung, may be used with the words of this hymn.)

---

1. "Church Triumphant," by S. Ralph Harlow. Used by permission of the author.

SERVICE 19

TEMPLE BUILDERS

Preparing To Build

MUSICAL MEDITATION: "I Would Be True" or
"Give of Your Best to the Master"

POEM:

> Isn't it strange that princes and kings,
> And clowns that caper in sawdust rings,
> And common folks like you and me
> Are builders for Eternity?
>
> To each is given a bag of tools,
> A shapeless mass and a book of rules;
> And each must make, ere life is flown,
> A stumbling block or a stepping stone.
>
> —R. L. SHARPE

LEADER:

Selecting the Architect

The story is told of three men who were working on a building which was under construction. A passer-by stopped by the building and asked each of the three the same question, "What are you doing?" The first man replied, "Stone-cuttin.'" The second man smiled and said, "Puttin' in time until a better job comes along." The third man paused for a moment and then answered, *"I'm building a cathedral!"*

As men and women of today are busily engaged in constructing the temple of their lives, they might be compared to the three men of this story. Some never rise above the drudgery of "stone-cut-

tin' "; others are just "puttin' in time" with the hope that something big will turn up some day; while others, endowed with a
vision splendid, see that the building of a life may be the equiva-
lent to the erection of a cathedral—a temple fit for the presence
of the living God. There are still others who may be likened unto
the foolish man whom Jesus described, "which built his house upon
the sand: and the rain descended, and the floods came, and the
winds blew, and beat upon that house; and it fell: and great was
the fall of it" (Matthew 7:26-27). What kind of a temple are *you*
building today?

In the beginning of life's journey, many young people begin to
build their lives with plans and materials of their own making,
giving little thought to the firmness of the foundation or the worth
of the materials which they are using. They forget that as archi-
tects they are untrained and unskilled; that no building will be
beautiful or useful unless constructed under the guidance of a
skilled architect and according to the expert plan of his carefully
drawn blueprint. In wilful pride and self-sufficiency, they often shut
themselves within their self-made walls of stone, unwilling to share
the citadel of their hearts with Another. Then it is that *He* comes—
the Architect divine—and with tender, pleading voice, he seeks ad-
mittance, until with shame and sorrow, they open wide the door to
his majestic presence, and he comes in to dwell forevermore.

HYMN: "O Jesus, Thou Art Standing" (all stanzas)

LEADER:

This Architect divine comes to each of us amid the ruins of our
self-built houses of life and says to us: "Except the Lord build the
house, they labour in vain that build it" (Psalm 127:1). "Know ye
not that ye are the *temple of God,* and that the Spirit of God dwelleth in you?" (1 Corinthians 3:16). "The most High dwelleth not
in temples made with hands; . . . what house will ye build me?
saith the Lord" (Acts 7:48-49).

And looking into his face, so full of tenderness and compassion
and love, surely the only answer which we can bring to him is:

Reg —

I shall build up my house anew,
With sturdier roof and walls and floor . . .
A fairer dwelling, and more true,
Than served my soul before.

It was a shining place enough,
But God is an observant guest . . .
And every flaw in shoddy stuff
Were straightly manifest.

The timbers of a selfish heart
Will crumble at the wind's assault . . .
By no apology nor art
Could I defend the fault.

This masonry of little worth,
These rooms unfit for His degree,
The cheap penates on my hearth,
I can not let Him see . . .

Christ was a goodly carpenter:
His honest eye would pierce me through
With greater shame than I could bear . . .
I build my house anew![1]

—SARA HENDERSON HAY

SOLO: "O Master Workman of the Race" (stanza 2)   *omit*
(Tune: "Materna")

O Carpenter of Nazareth,
Builder of life divine,
Who shapeth man to God's own law,
Thyself the fair design.
Build us a tower of Christlike height,
That we the land may view,
And see like Thee our noblest work
Our Father's work to do.[2]

—JAY T. STOCKING

---

1. "Not Made With Hands," by Sara Henderson Hay (Mrs. Raymond Holden). From *Good Housekeeping*, April, 1935. Used by permission of the author.

2. From *The Pilgrim Hymnal*. Copyright, 1931, 1935, by The Pilgrim Press. Used by permission.

Counting the Cost

[handwritten: also]

LEADER:

Any builder must first sit down with his chosen architect and count the cost before beginning to build. Jesus himself said, "For which of you, intending to build a tower, sitteth not down first, and counteth the cost, whether he have sufficient to finish it? Lest haply, after he hath laid the foundation, and is not able to finish it, all that behold it begin to mock him, saying, This man began to build, and was not able to finish it" (Luke 14:28-30).

Yes, there is a cost—the master Architect presents his terms before he can go further with the building: "If any man will come after me, let him deny himself, and take up his cross daily, and follow me" (Luke 9:23). Have you counted the cost? If you have, you will be ready to say, "Wherever he leads, I'll go."

[handwritten: Solo by Helen]

HYMN: "Wherever He Leads I'll Go" (stanzas 1, 4), or "Where He Leads Me" (stanza 1 and refrain)

Securing the Blueprint

LEADER:

Having counted the cost and chosen to follow the master Architect, we must next go to him for the blueprint of our building. His plans are perfect, and he has a blueprint perfected for every one of his children. We have only to say, "Have thine own way, Lord," and he will reveal to us his plan and build of our lives temples which will reflect his glory.

[handwritten: omit]

HYMN: "Have Thine Own Way, Lord" (stanzas 1, 4)

POEM:

> . . . Ah, now, we know
> What it will cost—but our sufficiency
> Is God's own grace. The tower we build must grow,
> Upward and outward, a pulsating thing
> Alive and warm and beautiful, to stand

Eternal in the heavens; it must bring
God's love, like healing rain, to the parched land.
As high as heaven is above the earth.
So must we build a living citadel
Of Faith, life, love, prayer, and angelic mirth
Whose Cornerstone is Christ, Emmanuel.[3]

—BEVERLY GITHENS

PRAYER:

That Christ will be the Architect divine of our temple building, and teach us to erect a temple which will be a fit dwelling place for the Spirit of the living God.

---

3. From "Builders," by Beverly Githens. *Clear Horizons Magazine,* July, 1944.

SERVICE 20

TEMPLE BUILDERS

Erecting the Temple

MUSICAL MEDITATION: "Higher Ground," or
"O Jesus, I Have Promised"

POEM:

We are building every day
In a good or evil way,
And the structure, as it grows,
Will our inmost self disclose,

Till in every arch and line
All our faults and failings shine;
It may grow a castle grand,
Or a wreck upon the sand.

Do you ask what building this
That can show both pain and bliss,
That can be both dark and fair?
Lo, its name is character!

Build it well, whate'er you do;
Build it straight and strong and true;
Build it clear and high and broad;
Build it for the eye of God.

—I. E. DICKENGA

Laying the Foundation

LEADER:

The first step in the building of any house is the laying of its foundation. The master Architect tells us very clearly what we must use as our foundation if our building is to stand: "For other foundation can no man lay than that is laid, which is Jesus Christ" (1 Corinthians 3:11).

HYMN: "How Firm a Foundation" (stanzas 1, 5)

Placing the Cornerstone

LEADER:

The placing of the cornerstone in any building is always a ceremony of sacred significance. And all important is the laying of the cornerstone in our temple of life, for there is only One who is worthy of such a place of honor and distinction: "The stone which the builders rejected, the same is become the head of the corner" (Luke 20:17). "Jesus Christ himself being the chief cornerstone; in whom all the building fitly framed together groweth unto an holy temple in the Lord: in whom ye also are builded together for a habitation of God through the Spirit" (Ephesians 2:20-22).

HYMN: "My Hope Is Built on Nothing Less" (stanzas 1, 3)

Selecting the Materials

LEADER:

The master Architect also suggests that there are various materials which we may use to build upon our foundation. "Now if any man build upon this foundation gold, silver, precious stones, wood, hay, stubble; every man's work shall be made manifest: for the day shall declare it, because it shall be revealed by fire; and the fire shall try every man's work of what sort it is. If any man's work abide which he hath built thereupon, he shall receive a reward. If any man's work shall be burned, he shall suffer loss: but he himself shall be saved; yet so as by fire" (1 Corinthians 3:12-15).

These materials are offered us: gold, silver, precious stones, wood, hay, stubble. Which will we choose? If we build with the materials suggested in this song, surely the master Architect will crown our task with his approval when our final work is made manifest.

SOLO: "My Task"—Ashford, or

HYMN: "Our Best"

Hewing the Windows

LEADER:

Windows must be hewn in the walls of our building that the sunlight of God's presence may shine within our temple of life to broaden and clarify our vision.

> I will hew great windows for my soul,
> Channels of splendor, portals of release;
>
> . . . .
>
> That the *being* of me have room to grow,
> That my eyes may meet God's eyes and know,
> I will hew great windows, wonderful windows, measureless
>   windows for my soul.[1]
>
> —ANGELA MORGAN

HYMN: "Open My Eyes, That I May See" (stanza 1)

LEADER:

Placing the Roof

No building would be complete without a roof to serve as shelter from the storms that beat upon and threaten to wreck our temple of life. Such a temple as we are erecting will need a roof whose lofty pinnacles will reach unto the heights of heaven itself. And so we build our roof of *prayer*, the only channel through which we may reach heavenward and find ourselves very "near to the heart of God."

SOLO OR QUARTET: "Near to the Heart of God"

(After the second stanza, the soloist or quartet continues to hum the hymn through a period of silent meditation and prayer.)

ORGAN OR PIANO: (Tune: "Finlandia")

(Play softly through the reading of the first two stanzas of the following poem; soloist or quartet then sings the last stanza to above tune.)

---

1. From "Room," by Angela Morgan. Permission granted by the author.

We would be building; temples still undone
O'er crumbling walls their crosses scarcely lift;
Waiting till love can raise the broken stone,
And hearts creative bridge the human rift;
We would be building, Master, let Thy plan
Reveal the life that God would give to man.

Teach us to build; upon the solid rock
We set the dream that hardens into deed,
Ribbed with the steel that time and change doth mock,
Th' unfailing purpose of our noblest creed;
Teach us to build; O Master, lend us sight
To see the towers gleaming in the light.

O keep us building, Master; may our hands
Ne'er falter when the dream is in our hearts,
When to our ears there come divine commands
And all the pride of sinful will departs;
We build with Thee, O grant enduring worth
Until the heav'nly Kingdom comes on earth.[2]

—Purd E. Deitz

PRAYER:

O Master, may our finished creation be a life full of goodness and beauty, a temple fit for the presence of the living God. For we ask it in Jesus' name. Amen.

---

2. "We Would Be Building," by Purd E. Deitz. Used by permission of the author.

SERVICE 21

"THE KING IN HIS BEAUTY"

"Jesus Christ, the Same Yesterday"

MUSICAL MEDITATION: "Majestic Sweetness Sits Enthroned"
(Continue playing throughout the following
reading)

SCRIPTURE READING:

"Thine eyes shall see the King in his beauty" (Isaiah 33:17).
"And when we shall see him, there is no beauty that we should desire him" (Isaiah 53:2). "For how great is his goodness, and how
great is his beauty!" (Zechariah 9:17).

POEM:

"The King in His beauty,"—say, who could He be?
The Saviour who suffered and died on the tree?
The One who companions each step of today,
And whispers His promise, "I'm with you always"?
Or is He the King who is reigning above,
Who one day shall rule in His Kingdom of Love?
Say, who is this "King in His beauty," I pray,
Could He be the Jesus of God's Yesterday?
Or is He the Presence I feel all the while
As I travel Life's journey mile after mile?
And sweet is the answer, thrilling my soul,
This "King in His beauty" o'er *all* has control—
For He's Jesus the Christ, the same *yesterday*,
And *today*, and *forever*—what more could I say?

ZULA E. COON

SOLO (sung by concealed soloist): "Majestic Sweetness Sits Enthroned" (stanzas 1, 2)

LEADER:

"Jesus Christ, the same *yesterday*." How may we see the "King in his beauty" in this Jesus of yesterday?

1ST READER:

In the beginning there was a "King in his beauty" who was with God and who *was* God, and this "King in his beauty" was "made flesh and dwelt among us, and we beheld his glory, the glory as of the only begotten of the Father, full of grace and truth" (John 1:14).

> To Him all life was beauty. The sun upon the hills,
> The sweeping shadows, and the winding lane.
> Morning He loved, with dewdrops on the flowers;
> Evening, with sunset and soft, warm April rain.
> Friends He found in lepers stumbling to Him,
> Love in those who hate, grace in sinners' eyes.
> Dawn He saw with all earth's new-born glory,
> Twilight and darkness, and hope in human sighs.
> Youth was His, and springtime, and music in the trees;
> Life was His, and sunshine, and the murmuring of the bees.
> Joy in healing broken hearts; manhood's noble strife;
> All the wonder and the beauty of a sacred human life.
>
> . . . .
>
> He walked the common lanes, the city streets He trod,
> And in His heart was beauty. . . the beauty born of God.[1]

—A. L. C.

SOLO: "The Stranger of Galilee"—Morris (stanza 1 and refrain)

2ND READER:

> How beauteous were the marks divine,
>   That in Thy meekness used to shine,
> That lit Thy lonely pathway, trod
>   In wondrous love, O Son of God!
>
> O who like Thee, so calm, so bright,
>   Lord Jesus Christ, thou Light of light;
> O who like Thee did ever go
>   So patient through a world of woe?

---

1. From *The Master of Men,* Richard R. Smith, publishers, 1930. Used by permission of Thomas Curtis Clark.

O who like Thee so humbly bore
　The scorn, the scoffs of men, before;
So meek, so lowly, yet so high,
　So glorious in humility?

Through all Thy life-long weary years,
　A Man of sorrows and of tears,
The cross, where all our sins were laid,
　Upon Thy bending shoulders weighed;

And death, that sets the prisoner free,
　Was pang and scoff and scorn to Thee;
Yet love through all Thy torture glowed,
And mercy with Thy life-blood flowed.

　　　　　　　　—ARTHUR CLEVELAND COXE

HYMN: "There is a Green Hill Far Away" (stanzas 1, 2, 3), or
　　"He Died of a Broken Heart" (stanzas 1, 2, 3)

3RD READER:

　　　　　　　　He died!
And with Him perished all that men hold dear;
Hope lay beside Him in the sepulcher,
Love grew corse cold, and all things beautiful beside
　Died when He died.

　　　　　　　　He rose!
And with Him hope arose, and life and light.
Men said, "Not Christ but Death died yesternight."
And joy and truth and all things virtuous
　Rose when He rose.

　　　　　　　　—AUTHOR UNKNOWN

HYMN: "Christ Arose" (stanzas 1, 3)

PRAYER (by leader): Of thanksgiving for the "King in his beauty"
as revealed to us in the Jesus of yesterday.

SERVICE 22

"THE KING IN HIS BEAUTY"

"Jesus Christ, the Same Today"

MUSICAL MEDITATION: "Majestic Sweetness Sits Enthroned"
(Continue playing throughout the following
reading.)

SCRIPTURE READING:

Use Scripture reading in introduction to Service 21, "Jesus
Christ, the Same Yesterday."

POEM:

Use poem in introduction to Service 21, "Jesus Christ, the Same
Yesterday."

SOLO (sung by concealed soloist): "Majestic Sweetness Sits Enthroned" (stanzas 1, 4)

LEADER:

"Jesus Christ, the same *today*." How may we see the "King in
his beauty" in this Jesus of today?

1ST READER:

This "King in his beauty" reveals himself to us today as we look
upon the beauty of nature, for "the heavens declare his righteousness, and all the people see his glory" (Psalm 97:6).

> God is not far from any one of us:
> The wild flower by the wayside speaks His love;
> Each blithesome bird bears tidings from above;
> Sunshine and shower His tender mercies prove,
> And men know not His voice!

God is not far from any one of us:
  He speaks to us in every glad sunrise;
  His glory floods us from the noonday skies;
  The stars declare His love when daylight dies,
    And men know not His voice![1]

—Thomas Curtis Clark

Hymn: "Fairest Lord Jesus" (all stanzas)

2nd Reader:

Jesus' parting promise to his disciples was that he would return
to live within them as the Spirit of truth. "And I will pray the
Father, and he shall give you another Comforter, that he may abide
with you for ever; even the Spirit of truth; whom the world cannot receive, because it seeth him not, neither knoweth him: but ye
know him; for he dwelleth with you, and shall be in you. I will
not leave you comfortless: I will come to you" (John 14:16-18).

O Son of Man, who walked each day
  A humble road, serene and strong,
Go with me now upon life's way,
  My Comrade all the journey long.

If light and joy should be my part,
  Then share with me the shining hour;
If clouds should come, speak to my heart
  Thy word of comfort, love, and power.

So shall I walk in happiness,
  So shall my task with love be fraught—
If thou art near to mark and bless
  The labor done, the beauty wrought.

O Son of God, who came and shed
  A light for all the ages long,
Thy company shall make me glad,
  Thy fellowship shall keep me strong.[2]

—Nancy Byrd Turner

1. From "God Is Not Far," from *God's Dreams*, by Thomas Curtis Clark; Willett, Clark
& Co., 1943. Used by permission of the author.

2. From *Hymnal for Youth*. Copyright, 1949, published by the Westminster Press.
Used by permission.

HYMN: "Close to Thee" (stanzas 1, 2), or

SOLO OR QUARTET: "I'd Rather Have Jesus"

3RD READER:

"When it comes to Jesus of Nazareth, in the midst of the founders of other religions, there is absolutely no apology, no compromise, no comparison. He towers above them as the snow-capped peaks of the Himalayas tower in regal majesty above the foothills round about. He is the same blessed Jesus whose feet pressed the sands of the shores of Galilee nineteen hundred years ago. He is the same inspiring teacher whose lips phrased those potent sentences which marked him as one having authority and not as the scribes. . . . He is the same suffering Saviour who bled upon the cross and died for the sins of the world; and by the same token, he is the same conquering King who broke the bonds of death and came forth from the tomb clad in his spotless robes of immortality, pure as the spray as it dances in the sunlight in the morning, and ready to ascend into the presence of the Father, that he might assume his throne and his scepter. Jesus, the same yesterday, today, and forever is always 'the power of God unto salvation to everyone who believes.' He is unchanging and unchangeable in his power to redeem." (Author Unknown)

HYMN: "My Redeemer" (stanzas 1, 2, 3), or
"How Sweet the Name of Jesus" (all stanzas), or
"Jesus, the Very Thought of Thee" (all stanzas)

PRAYER:

Of thanksgiving for the "Jesus of Today," who is "the power of God unto salvation to everyone who believes."

SERVICE 23

"THE KING IN HIS BEAUTY"

"Jesus Christ, the Same Forever"

MUSICAL MEDITATION: "Majestic Sweetness Sits Enthroned"
(Continue playing throughout the following
reading)

SCRIPTURE READING:

Use Scripture reading in introduction to Service 21, "Jesus Christ,
the Same Yesterday."

POEM:

Use poem in introduction to Service 21, "Jesus Christ, the Same
Yesterday."

SOLO (sung by concealed soloist): "Majestic Sweetness Sits Enthroned" (stanzas 1, 2)

LEADER:

"Jesus Christ, the same *forever.*" How shall we see the "King in
his beauty" in this Jesus of forever?

1ST READER:

"And I beheld, and I heard the voice of many angels round about
the throne and the beasts and the elders: and the number of them
was ten thousand times ten thousand, and thousands of thousands;
saying with a loud voice, Worthy is the Lamb that was slain to receive power, and riches, and wisdom, and strength, and honour, and
glory, and blessing. And every creature which is in heaven, and on
the earth, and under the earth, and such as are in the sea, and all
that are in them, heard I saying, Blessing and honour, and glory,

and power, be unto him that sitteth upon the throne, and unto the
Lamb for ever and ever" (Revelation 5:11-13).

HYMN: "Hark, Ten Thousand Harps and Voices" (stanzas 1, 3,
     4), or
     "Jesus Shall Reign Where'er the Sun" (stanzas 1, 3, 4)

2ND READER:

Yes, Jesus, the "King in his beauty" *shall* reign; his kingdom
shall continue to spread through all the world until he comes again
in all his glory.

> Thou art coming, Thou art coming!
>   We shall meet Thee on Thy way,
> We shall see Thee, we shall know Thee,
> We shall bless Thee, we shall show Thee
>   All our hearts could never say!
> What an anthem that will be,
> Ringing out our love to Thee,
> Pouring out our rapture sweet
>   At Thine own all-glorious feet!
>
> O the joy to see Thee reigning,
>   Thee, my own beloved Lord!
> Every tongue Thy Name confessing,
> Worship, honor, glory, blessing,
>   Brought to Thee with glad accord!
> Thee, my Master and my Friend,
>   Vindicated and enthroned!
> Unto earth's remotest end,
>   Glorified, adored, and owned!
>
>   —FRANCES R. HAVERGAL

HYMN: "It May Be at Morn" (stanzas 1, 4)

3RD READER:

> When that inevitable hour shall come,
> When shadows all have lengthened
> To the end,
> Lights are all dim—
> What will you do, my soul,
> In that great hour of waiting
> Without Him?

Yea, without Him?
Who was in the beginning,
Who flung the morning stars
Upon their way—
Yea, without Him,
The light, the life eternal,
Who watches to the closing
Of the day?

"Come unto me," He cries;
Nor can I fail Him!
And shadows grow
And lengthen to the end,
And lights are dim—
What hope is there, my soul,
In that great hour of waiting
Without Him?[1]

—RALPH SPAULDING CUSHMAN

(Invitation may be given here if desired.)

HYMN: "Will Jesus Find Us Watching?" (sing slowly and softly)

LEADER:

Worthy indeed is this "King in his beauty" who sits upon his throne to be crowned the King of our hearts and lives; worthy indeed is his name to be proclaimed to men and women of every race and creed the world over! Let us renew our consecration to this "King in his beauty" and proclaim his name in love and life wherever we are, until the voices of the redeemed shall rise in one great paean of praise to crown him—*Jesus Christ, the same yesterday, today, and forever*—Lord of all!

HYMN: "All Hail the Power" (all stanzas), or
      "Crown Him with Many Crowns" (all stanzas)

PRAYER (leader):

Of thanksgiving for the "King in his beauty" as he has been revealed to us in the Jesus of yesterday, as he daily reveals himself

---

1. "The Inevitable Hour," from *Practicing The Presence* by Ralph S. Cushman, Copyright, 1936, by Ralph S. Cushman. By permission of Abingdon-Cokesbury Press.

to us in the Jesus of today, and as he shall be revealed in the Jesus of forever.

SUGGESTIONS FOR CARRYING OUT THESE SERVICES:

A concealed soloist or quartet could be used for all the musical numbers of these services until the last hymn, which should be sung by the entire group.

If a large picture of the head of Christ can be secured, have it placed where it may be seen by the group throughout the services. If used for evening services, a light upon the picture would add to its effectiveness.

SERVICE 24

VISION + VIM = VICTORY

Vision

MUSICAL MEDITATION: "Open My Eyes, That I May See"

OPENING MEDITATION:

Youth, O Youth, can I reach you,
    Can I speak and make you hear?
Can I open your eyes to see me?
    Can my presence draw you near?

Is there a prophet among you,
    One with a heart to know?
I will flash my secrets on him,
    He shall watch my glory grow.

For I, the God, the Father,
    The Quest, the Final Goal,
Still search for a prophet among you,
    To speak my word to his soul.

—ANONYMOUS

LEADER:

All the great prophets and apostles of the long ago began their ministry by seeing a vision and then translating that vision into action. Let us note the vision which came to one of these prophets of the past.

We open the book of Isaiah, and there we read: "The vision of Isaiah . . . which he saw." What was this vision which Isaiah saw? First, he saw his country of Judah with all its selfishness and sin, its national pride, its indifference to spiritual values. If his vision had stopped there, discouragement and frustration would have been the result, but as we look on into the sixth chapter, we read where he says, *"I saw also the Lord."* Isaiah looked *above* and *beyond* the conditions of the world in which he lived and "saw also the Lord, sitting upon a throne, high and lifted up," and his response was, "Here am I; send me."

Every youth, facing the beginning of life, needs to have his eyes opened to the vision which the Lord would have him see. What is this vision which youth needs to see? First of all, and most needful, he must open his eyes to see *the Lord*—Christ Jesus, lifted up on a cross of shame. Having caught such a vision of the Christ of the cross, it must follow that he shall see *his own self* in the light of Christ's revealing Spirit.

The first thing which Isaiah saw as he came into the presence of the Lord was his own sinful self, and he cried out, "Woe is me! for I am undone; because I am a man of unclean lips, . . . for mine eyes have seen the King, the Lord of hosts." After this confession came the cleansing fire of purification, through which he was cleansed and made ready for God's commission.

Following any young person's first vision of Christ, there must be also a searching of heart, a cleansing of life, a resolution to surrender all else in order to receive the high calling of God in Christ Jesus.

This revelation of self with its accompanying cleansing and consecration shall come as one waits "in deep mid-silence, open-doored to God."

> If the chosen soul could never be alone
> In deep mid-silence, open-doored to God,
> No greatness ever had been dreamed or done,
> Among dull hearts a prophet never grew;
> The nurse of full-grown souls is solitude.
>
> —JAMES RUSSELL LOWELL

HYMN: "Open My Eyes, That I May See" (stanza 1)

LEADER:

What other vision does youth need to see before the vision is complete? He needs to see *world need* and his relationship to it.

As Isaiah gazed upon the vision of the Lord "high and lifted up," he saw not only his own sinful self, but he saw also that he dwelt "in the midst of a people of unclean lips."

As you wait upon the Lord, he will also open your eyes and your ears to see and hear the needs of your brothers near and far, and you will find that your vision will broaden to include, not a narrow circle of selfish dreams, but an ever-enlarging vision of *God's dreams*. His dreams for his world shall become your dreams, and you will hear his call to have a part in the fulfilment of those dreams.

> Dreams are they—but they are God's dreams!
> Shall we decry them and scorn them?
> That men shall love one another,
> That white shall call black man brother,
> That greed shall pass from the market-place,
> That lust shall yield to love for the race,
> That man shall meet with God face to face—
> Dreams are they all,
>   But shall we despise them—
>   God's dreams!
>
> Dreams are they—to become man's dreams!
> Can we say nay as they claim us?
> That men shall cease from their hating,
> That war shall soon be abating.
> That the glory of kings and lords shall pale,
> That the pride of dominion and power shall fail,
> That the love of humanity shall prevail—
> Dreams are they all,
>   But shall we despise them—
>   God's dreams![1]
>
> —THOMAS CURTIS CLARK

HYMN: "Open My Eyes, That I May See" (stanza 2)

LEADER:

As the cleansing fire of the Lord touched Isaiah's lips, then was he purified and made fit for the Master's use. Only then was he worthy to bear the truth of God's message to a needy world, to translate his vision into action.

---

1. "God's Dreams," by Thomas Curtis Clark. From *1000 Quotable Poems*, Harper & Brothers, 1937. Used by permission of the author.

Thus, you must wait God's cleansing, that your lips, too, may be worthy to "bear the warm truth everywhere."

HYMN: "Open My Eyes, That I May See" (stanza 3)

LEADER:

Having received the vision, may you be able to say with Paul, "I was not disobedient unto the heavenly vision" (Acts 26:19).

Let us pray:

PRAYER-POEM:

> God—let me be aware.
> Let me not stumble blindly down the ways,
> Just getting somehow safely through the days,
> Not even groping for another hand,
> Not even wondering why it all was planned,
> Eyes to the ground unseeking for the light,
> Soul never aching for a wild-winged flight,
> Please, keep me eager just to do my share.
> God—let me be aware.
>
> God—let me be aware.
> Stab my soul fiercely with others' pain,
> Let me walk seeing horror and stain.
> Let my hands, groping, find other hands.
> Give me the heart that divines, understands.
> Give me the courage, wounded, to fight.
> Flood me with knowledge, drench me in light.
> Please, keep me eager just to do my share.
> God—let me be aware.

—MIRIAM TEICHNER

HYMN: "Lord, Speak to Me That I May Speak"

SERVICE 25

VISION + VIM = VICTORY

Vim

MUSICAL MEDITATION: "Arise, O Youth of God"

OPENING MEDITATION:

> Make my mortal dreams come true
>   With the work I fain would do;
> Clothe with life the weak intent,
>   Let me be the thing I meant;
> Let me find in Thy employ,
>   Peace that dearer is than joy.

—JOHN GREENLEAF WHITTIER

LEADER:

Vim is that force or vitality in man which translates his dreams and visions into reality.

> Dreams grow holy put in action,
> Work grows fair through starry dreaming.

—ADELAIDE PROCTER

One is needful to the other; to have vision without vim is to become a mere fanciful dreamer; to work without vision turns work into mere drudgery.

If Isaiah had turned from his vision of the Lord to spend the rest of his life contemplating the wonder and beauty of his vision, he would have gone down in history as an unknown dreamer who became the victim rather than the vitalizer of his vision. But instead, the vision called forth a ready response, "Here am I; send me" which sent him forth as the fearless prophet and heralder of the coming King.

Youth, too, may see the Lord; he may catch a vision of the high calling of God in Christ Jesus which comes in the light of that revelation; but unless he puts aside lesser things to serve the King of kings, the vision will be of little value.

> Go, labor on! spend and be spent;
> Thy joy to do the Father's will:
> It is the way the Master went—
> Should not the servant tread it still?[1]

HYMN: "Arise, O Youth of God" (stanza 1)

LEADER:

Youth may dream God's dreams of righting the wrong, of winning the lost, of helping to bring God's kingdom upon earth, but unless he begins by righting the wrong in his own household, unless he goes to his own lost friend or neighbor with the story of Jesus, unless he seeks to bring God's kingdom into his own community, there is little likelihood that God's dreams shall become reality.

> Go, labor on! 'tis not for naught,
> Thine earthly loss is heavenly gain;
> Men heed thee, love thee, praise thee not;
> The Master praises—what are men?

HYMN: "Arise, O Youth of God" (stanza 2)

LEADER:

Youth may catch a glimpse of the needs of his church—of its inadequate program of worship, of its failure to make its voice a telling one for Christ in his community. And yet if he comes to its sanctuary in a spirit and attitude which helps to destroy rather than to create worship, if he refuses to render service to his Master through the church, if he fails to support his church in word and deed and prayer, then the needs of his church will multiply rather than be lessened.

---

1. Horatius Bonar; also three following stanzas.

> Go, labor on, while it is day;
> The world's dark night is hastening on:
> Speed, speed thy work, cast sloth away;
> It is not thus that souls are won.

HYMN: "Arise, O Youth of God" (stanza 3)

LEADER:

Yes, vision must be coupled with vim if God's kingdom is to come on earth as it is in heaven. And it is to the youth of every land that God has sent his clarion call of challenge:

> Toil on, faint not, keep watch and pray, ·
> Be wise the erring soul to win;
> Go forth into the world's highway;
> Compel the wanderer to come in.

HYMN: "Arise, O Youth of God" (stanza 4)

LEADER:

> A Vision without a Task is a dream;
> A Task without a Vision is Drudgery;
> A Vision and a Task are the hope of the world.

> —ANONYMOUS

Are you willing and ready to say, "Here am I; send me?"

HYMN: "Hark, the Voice of Jesus Calling"

PRAYER:

"Our Father God, we thank Thee for the time in which we live; that our day is in a wonderful way Thy day, that the scope of fruitful activity is wide and varied, furnishing a place for service for each of us and a use for every talent. We rejoice that the highest and holiest interests are offered for our attention and activity. Forbid that we should live dumbly in the presence of these. 'Take the dimness of our souls away.' 'Stab our spirits broad awake.' Make us aware. By the inspiration of Thy Holy Spirit, may we have the insight to follow Thy truest prophets in our day and discern Thy way through the world. We would know the signs of the times and have the resolution to be constant in our devotion to the causes which make for justice and righteousness. So shall we be one with Thee and with all others of Thy servants in bringing Thy Kingdom, for Jesus' sake. Amen."[2]

---

2. By Mrs. B. W. Lipscomb, from *The Book of Daily Devotion,* edited by Clark and Cram. Copyright, 1932, by Whitmore & Smith. By permission of Abingdon-Cokesbury Press.

SERVICE 26

VISION + VIM = VICTORY

Victory

MUSICAL MEDITATION: "Awake, My Soul, Stretch Every Nerve"

OPENING MEDITATION:

> Great it is to believe the dream
> As we stand in youth by the starry stream;
> But a greater thing is to fight life through
> And say at the end, "The dream is true!"[1]
>
> —EDWIN MARKHAM

LEADER:

For those of us who possess and utilize this happy combination, vision plus vim, life becomes a victorious adventure. Vision + Vim = Victory!

"We are more than conquerors through him that loved us" (Romans 8:37). Let us always remember that the secret of victory is found in these words: "Through him that loved us." Vision and vim—*without Christ*—will not bring victory; vision and vim, consecrated to and impelled by his Spirit, make us "more than conquerors!"

Someone has said that one of the most dangerous heresies in the world today is the emphasis that is being given by professing Christians on *what we do for God* rather than on *what God does through us*.

Alone, we cannot catch a vision of Christ or of the task to which he calls us, but beholding the vision through his eyes will open our eyes to visions and aspirations hitherto unknown.

---

1. Used by permission of Virgil Markham.

Alone, we cannot have the vim or the ability to translate our dreams into action, but "through him that loved us" we shall be increasingly amazed at what we are able to accomplish.

Alone, we can never attain the victory, but with him "we are more than conquerors!"

Therefore, "forgetting those things which are behind, and reaching forth unto those things which are before," let us "press toward the mark for the prize of the high calling of God in Christ Jesus" (Philippians 3:13-14).

HYMN: "Awake, My Soul, Stretch Every Nerve" (stanza 1)

LEADER:

"Wherefore seeing we also are compassed about with so great a cloud of witnesses, let us lay aside every weight, and the sin which doth so easily beset us, and let us run with patience the race that is set before us, looking unto Jesus the author and finisher of our faith; who for the joy that was set before him endured the cross, despising the shame, and is set down at the right hand of the throne of God" (Hebrews 12:1-2).

HYMN: "Awake, My Soul, Stretch Every Nerve" (stanza 2)

LEADER:

"Know ye not that they which run in a race run all, but one receiveth the prize? So run, that ye may obtain" (1 Corinthians 9:24).

HYMN: "Awake, My Soul, Stretch Every Nerve" (stanza 3)

LEADER:

"I have fought a good fight, I have finished my course, I have kept the faith: henceforth there is laid up for me a crown of righteousness, which the Lord, the righteous judge, shall give me at that day: and not to me only, but unto all them also that love his appearing" (2 Timothy 4:7-8).

HYMN: "Awake, My Soul, Stretch Every Nerve" (stanza 4)

LEADER:

"But thanks be to God, which giveth us the victory through our Lord Jesus Christ" (1 Corinthians 15:57).

HYMN: "Stand Up, My Soul, Shake Off Thy Fears" (Tune: "Duke Street")

Words:

Stand up, my soul, shake off thy fears,
And gird the gospel armor on;
March to the gates of endless joy,
Where Jesus, thy great Captain's gone.

Hell and thy sins resist thy course;
But hell and sin are vanquished foes;
Thy Saviour nailed them to the cross
And sung the triumph when he rose.

Then let my soul march boldly on,
Press forward to the heav'nly gate;
There peace and joy eternal reign,
And glitt'ring robes for conqu'rors wait.

There shall I wear a starry crown,
And triumph in almighty grace,
While all the armies of the skies
Join in my glorious Leader's praise.

—ISAAC WATTS

DIRECTED PRAYER: (leader)

Our Father, we thank Thee for the ever-enlarging vision which comes to us, thy children, as we look up to the Christ of the cross.

(Pause for silent prayer.)

Open our eyes that we may see ourselves as Thou dost see us, that through that vision we may rise above our selfish, sinful selves to become worthy of our high calling as children of the King.

(Pause for silent prayer.)

Open our ears to the cries of our brothers in distress, both near and far, that we may reach out eager hands and hearts to lift them unto Thee.

(Pause for silent prayer.)

Give us the will to work for Thee unceasingly; give us the vim to translate our visions into action.

(Pause for silent prayer.)

Keep us obedient to the "heavenly vision" which Thou didst give us when we first found the Lord, that we may know the victory that comes to those who put their trust in Thee; for "this is the victory that overcometh the world, even our faith" (1 John 5:4).

(Pause for silent prayer.)

This we ask in Jesus' name. Amen.

PRAYER BEFORE SINGING

A song is a beautiful thing!
Voices join in full-throated melody,
And lift to blend in glorious harmony.
Men's hearts are moved, e'en lifted to ecstasy
With a song; for a song is a beautiful thing!

But when I sing, Lord,
Let it not be for this alone,
Lest fruitless I be when day is gone;
Touch Thou my lips; Thy beauty let me see,
And fill my heart with love eternally,
That men may come to know and adore Thee:
Lord, this prayer I bring;
Lord, for Thee I sing![2]

—Don Hustad

2. Used by permission of the author and the Moody Chorale.

PART II

SERVICES IN SONG

FOR

SPECIAL OCCASIONS

SERVICE 27

ANOTHER YEAR IS DAWNING

(A Service for the New Year)

SOLO OR QUARTET: "Another Year Is Dawning" (all stanzas)
(Tune: "Aurelia")

Another year is dawning,
Dear Father, let it be
In working and in waiting
Another year with Thee;
Another year of progress,
Another year of praise,
Another year of proving
Thy presence all the days.

Another year of mercies,
Of faithfulness and grace,
Another year of gladness
In the shining of Thy face;
Another year of leaning
Upon Thy loving breast,
Another year of trusting,
Of quiet, happy rest.

Another year of service,
Of witness of Thy love,
Another year of training
For holier work above;
Another year is dawning,
Dear Father, let it be
On earth, or else in heaven,
Another year for Thee.

—FRANCES R. HAVERGAL

READING: (Music of above hymn played softly throughout reading)

"I am the New Year.

"I am the one unspoiled bit of beauty in God's universe.

"I am romance, and glitter, and high resolution, and—dreams.

"My only handicap is the dead weight of old habits and hard-set ways of doing things that I must carry over from the past into my new ministry to your heart.

"My one fear is that someday you also will settle down to the conviction that the new is always an illusion.

"My single hope lies in your deepening faith,

"Faith that what has been proved impossible by long experience can at last be attained;

"Faith that failure is but an incident and not the end of the journey;

"Faith that someday mankind will be free from the shackles of his own forging, childhood will have its chance, and love will achieve its Godlike destiny;

"Faith that he who said, "Behold, I make all things new" had somehow grasped the secret for making his own dream come true.

"Faith that those who share with him the adventure of his self-commitment shall find the secret of overflowing life.

"I am God's plan for girding the loins of his intrepid co-workers in the long, but joyous march to the goal of his beneficent purpose.

"I am the New Year."[1]

PRAYER: For guidance and faith sufficient to meet the adventure of the New Year.

LEADER:

"The land, whither ye go to possess it, is a land of hills and valleys, and drinketh water of the rain of heaven: a land which the Lord thy God careth for: the eyes of the Lord thy God are always upon it, from the beginning of the year even unto the end of the year" (Deuteronomy 11:11-12).

---

1. From *The Baptist Student*, January 1948.

Today each one of us faces the challenge of a new year; yet not one of us may know just what experiences, what changes, what joys or sorrows await us along the path of 19——. It is a land of hills and valleys which we go to possess, for some days may hold mountaintop experiences, while others may find us traveling through valleys of discouragement or sorrow or need. But the glad message which this verse brings to us is this: *The Lord thy God careth for it; his eyes are upon it even unto the end of the year.*

HYMN: "God Will Take Care of You" (all stanzas)

LEADER:

The future stands before us, veiled in mystery, but we have the blessed assurance that Christ, our Good Shepherd, *goeth on before.*

"Whatever awaits us is encountered first by Him. Faith's eye can always discern His majestic presence in front; and when that cannot be seen, it is dangerous to move forward. Bind this comfort to your heart, that the Saviour has tried for Himself all the experiences through which He asks you to pass; and He would not ask you to pass through them unless He was sure that they were not too difficult for your feet or too trying for your strength."[2]

HYMN: "He Leadeth Me" (all stanzas)

LEADER:

One lesson which our Saviour would teach us is to travel only *one step at a time.* So often we would try to run ahead to see what lies on the trail far beyond; but he would draw us back and teach us to live only one day at a time. Each day of 19——, well lived, will enrich our year and help to create an abundant and beautiful life.

> Listen to the Exhortation of the Dawn!
>> Look to this day!
> For it is Life, and the very Life of Life.
> In its brief course lie all the
>> Verities and Realities of your Existence;
>> The Bliss of Growth,

---

2. From *Streams in the Desert,* by Mrs. Charles E. Cowman. Copyright, 1925, Oriental Missionary Society, Los Angeles, Cal. Used by permission of the author.

The Glory of Action,
The Splendor of Beauty;
For Yesterday is but a Dream,
And Tomorrow is only a Vision;
But Today well lived makes
Every yesterday a Dream of Happiness,
And every Tomorrow a Vision of Hope.
Look well therefore to this Day!
Such is the salutation of the Dawn.

—From the SANSKRIT

SOLO: "Just for Today" (hymn arrangement), or
"Just for Today"—Abbott, or

HYMN: "Lord, for Tomorrow and Its Need"

LEADER:

Too many of us are fearful to venture forth to higher ground or
to reach for the stars. We drift about on the lowlands and refuse
to climb to that higher plane of living wherein the richest experiences in Christ are to be found. "Too low they build who build beneath the stars." (Edward Young)

Greatly begin! though thou have time
But for a line, be that sublime,—
Not failure, but low aim, is crime.

—JAMES RUSSELL LOWELL

May our prayer, our aim, this year be: "Lord, lead me on to
higher ground."

HYMN: "Higher Ground" (all stanzas)

PRAYER OF CONSECRATION FOR THE NEW YEAR

SERVICE 28

"WERE YOU THERE?"

(An Easter Service)

MUSICAL MEDITATION: "The Old Rugged Cross," or
                    "Beneath the Cross of Jesus"

SCRIPTURE READING: John 19:16-18

SOLO: "Were You There?" (Negro spiritual) (stanza 1)

> Were you there when they crucified my Lord?
> Oh, sometimes it causes me to tremble, brothers, tremble,
> Were you there when they crucified my Lord?

LEADER:

Into the lives of all of us who would fully surrender our all to
the Master, there must come a crucifixion time when we, too, must
bear our own smaller cross to a skull-shaped hill and know in part
the suffering and the sorrow of our Saviour. True, we cannot in
any measure know the fullness nor the depth of his sufferings, but
if we are to die to self and lose our lives completely in him, we
must face our own peculiar Calvaries. Those of us who would
render unto Christ the most sacrificial service must follow the blood-
stained pathway to Calvary's brow, and there let self be crucified
and slain in order that we may be able to say even as Paul, "I am
crucified with Christ: nevertheless I live; yet not I, but Christ liveth
in me" (Galatians 2:20).

With heads and hearts bowed, let us consider these words and
pray for strength to bear our crosses, whatever they may be:

Must Jesus bear the cross alone
And all the world go free?
No; there's a cross for every one,
And there's a cross for me.

The consecrated cross I'll bear
Till death shall set me free,
And then go home my crown to wear,
For there's a crown for me.

(Pianist plays the hymn slowly and quietly while leader reads the two stanzas, and continues to play after the reading for a brief period of silent meditation and prayer.)

SCRIPTURE READING: Matthew 27:57-60

SOLO: "Were You There?" (stanza 2)

Were you there when they laid Him in the tomb?
Oh, sometimes it causes me to tremble, brothers, tremble,
Were you there when they laid Him in the tomb?

LEADER:

In following our crucified Lord and Master, we must go even further and know the silence of the tomb if we are to rise to that new life of self-renunciation which brings freedom and deepest joy.

Let us bow again in the presence of the crucified, risen Christ as we pledge to him anew our willingness to follow him even into the silence of the tomb.

Oh, friend, we never choose the better part
Until we set the cross up in the heart.
I know I cannot live until I die,
Till I am nailed upon it, wild and high,
And sleep in the tomb for a full three days' dead
With angels at the feet and head.
But then, in a great brightness, shall I arise
To walk with stiller feet below the skies.[1]

—EDWIN MARKHAM

(Pianist plays "When I Survey the Wondrous Cross" while the above poem is read and continues playing during the period of silent prayer following. If preferred, the sacred solo of the above words may be substituted for the reading of the poem. The solo is entitled, "The Cross," by Harriet Ware.)

---

1. Used by permission of Virgil Markham.

SCRIPTURE READING: Matthew 28:1-6

SOLO: "Were You There?" (stanza 3)

> Were you there when He triumphed o'er the grave?
> Oh, sometimes it fills my soul with rapture, brothers, rapture,
> Were you there when He triumphed o'er the grave?

LEADER:

> Some of us stay at the cross,
>   Some of us wait at the tomb,
> Quickened and raised together with Christ,
>   Yet lingering still in its gloom.
>
> If the Christ who died had stopped at the cross,
>   His work had been incomplete;
> If the Christ who was buried had stayed in the tomb,
>   He had only known defeat;
>
> But the Way of the Cross never stops at the cross
>   And the Way of the Tomb leads on,
> To victorious grace in the heavenly place,
>   Where the risen Christ has gone.[2]

—ANNIE JOHNSON FLINT

Even as we turn our eyes away from the cross and the tomb at this Easter season to meditate upon the joyous reality of the resurrection, let us now turn our minds away from the crucifixion of self and the silence of the tomb to this glorious thought: that out of a Calvary, out of a sealed tomb, has come and will *always* come an Easter morning. The hope of the resurrection through the ages has been the hope that one day our physical bodies shall conquer death and the grave, and that we then shall be admitted into the living presence of our King of kings and Lord of lords. We do rejoice in this hope, but surely there is also another meaning in the resurrection message. Does it not also mean that after we die to self, after we pass through some great spiritual crisis into a higher realm of life, that there is an Easter morning for us even as we remain here on God's good earth? Even as the angel said to the women on that first Easter morning, "He is not here; he is risen," so Christ shall be able to look into our hearts and say, "Self

---

is no longer here. It is crucified and slain; and lo! *I* have arisen in you, to live forever in your heart and life!"

> There is fulfillment of the Easter promise
>   Not only in Eternity,
> But here and now to lonely, saddened hearts
>   Who know their smaller Calvaries.
>
> In better moments of desire and selfless longing,
>   We pray, "Let Self be crucified and slain"—
> The answer forms a cross, and, prayer forgotten,
>   We bear our irksome load with cries of pain.
>
> But crosses need not end with crucifixion;
>   The path leads onward, tinged with gloom,
> And those who pray for self-renunciation
>   Must follow Christ into the silent tomb.
>
> Yet fetters cannot hold a life surrendered;
>   There comes an Easter morning to the soul,
> When we arise, all scars and wounds transcending,
>   To find the living Christ has made us whole![3]

—Zula E. Coon

(Pianist plays the stanza of the hymn, "Christ Arose," slowly and softly several times through the reading of this poem. At the conclusion of the reading, the pianist should begin playing the refrain of "Christ Arose" while the whole congregation joins in the singing of it. This latter may be indicated by a sign from the song leader.)

Prayer:

Of thanksgiving for the risen Lord and for the hope of the resurrection which we have in him, now and forevermore.

---

3. From *I Quote*, by Virginia Ely. Copyright, 1947, George W. Stewart, Inc., publisher.

SERVICE 29

A SONG WAS BORN

(A Mother's Day Service)

MUSICAL MEDITATION: "Jesus, Saviour, Pilot Me"

(Pianist or organist plays this hymn once and continues to play through the reading of the following poem and prayer.)

POEM:

A song was born in the heart of a child
Through a mother's lullaby,
And the melody sweeter and sweeter grew
As the fleeting years passed by.

"Jesus—Saviour—Pilot me"—
The words brought quiet sleep,
But baby knew not of the Saviour dear
Who brought the slumber deep.

But the Saviour loved her, and, smiling,
Laid His Hand on the mother's heart,
To use her song, her love, her life,
A deeper peace to impart.

For "as a mother stills her child"
With a melody tender and low,
The child was led o'er Life's rough sea
By the Pilot she learned to know.

Your song and your life, oh, mother of mine,
Have guided me through the years,
For you gave me Jesus as Saviour and Friend,
God bless you and keep you, my dear.

ZULA E. COON

PRAYER OF GRATITUDE FOR ALL CHRISTIAN MOTHERS

LEADER:

How true it is that many of us have had a song implanted in our hearts through a mother's lullaby! Every true Christian mother is a singer of songs to her children, whether the song is sung with her voice, with her words, or with her life. Let us listen to some of the songs a mother may sing to her children—songs which echo in the heart of the child as long as life shall last.

1ST READER:

A song is born in the heart of a child through a mother's shining faith.

What can a mother give her children
Greater today than this one great thing—
Faith in an old, sweet, beautiful story,
A star—a stable—a new-born king?

Shining faith in the young lad, Jesus;
Lover of high white things was he:
Jesus—straight as a Lebanon cedar;
Jesus—clean as the winds from the sea.

Faith in the young lad come to manhood:
Jesus, compassionate, tender and true—
Oh, my children—what more glorious
Gift in the world can I give to you?

Carry it high like a lamp in the darkness,
Hold it for warmth when the day is cold—
Keep it for joy when youth goes singing,
Clasp it for peace when you are old.

What can a mother give her children
More than a faith that will not dim?
Take it, my dear ones—hold it forever:
A lamp for a lifetime—faith in him.[1]

—GRACE NOLL CROWELL

---

1. "The Beautiful Gift," from *Silver in the Sun* by Grace Noll Crowell (New York: Harper and Brothers, 1928, 1934). Used by permission.

HYMN: "Faith of Our Mothers" (Tune: "Faith of Our Fathers")

Faith of our mothers, living yet
    In cradle song and bedtime prayer,
In nursery love and fireside lore,
    Thy presence still pervades the air.
Faith of our mothers, living faith,
    We will be true to thee till death.

Faith of our mothers, lavish faith,
    The fount of childhood's trust and grace,
O may thy consecration prove
    The wellspring of a nobler race.
Faith of our mothers, lavish faith,
    We will be true to thee till death.

Faith of our mothers, guiding faith,
    For youthful longings—youthful doubts,
How blurred our vision, blind our way,
    Thy providential care without.
Faith of our mothers, guiding faith,
    We will be true to thee till death.

Faith of our mothers, Christian faith,
    In truth beyond our man-made creeds,
Still serve the home and save the church,
    And breathe thy spirit through our deeds.
Faith of our mothers, Christian faith,
    We will be true to thee till death.

—ARTHUR B. PATTEN

2ND READER:

A song was born in the heart of a child through a mother's steadfast love.

STORY:

"An angel once came to earth to garner for the museum of
Heaven the most beautiful and holy and sweetest things which this
earth knows. He came into a garden of rarest flowers. 'How beautiful!' thought the angel. 'These will add something to the fragrance
of Heaven!'

"Then he came to a sleeping child. As he bent over the little crib,
the baby smiled. 'Here,' whispered the angel, 'is something that all
my Heavenly comrades may well come near in silence to behold.'

"Then at last he came to a foul place filled with evil men. As one came out the angel followed him. He entered a home where a mother was waiting. She received him kindly. She ministered to him gently. As he slept, she stooped and left a kiss upon his brow. 'Ah,' said the angel, 'that is most like God.'

"The angel started on his flight back to the Holy City, bearing on his bosom three treasures—the perfume of the rose, the sweetness of the baby's smile, and the fervency of mother's love. When he came to the gates of Heaven he paused in his flight to take a peep at his precious treasures. But lo! the fragrance of the rose had vanished, the baby's smile was gone, but shining with the brightness of Heaven's throne, enduring as eternity, having absorbed within itself all the fragrance and the sweetness of the world, was left the mother's love. With a cry of joy the angel swept through the gates of pearl, bearing in his hands that which was to be the blessedness of Heaven as it had been the benediction of the earth."—AUTHOR UNKNOWN.

QUARTET: "O God, We Thank Thee"—Barnes, or

SOLO: "A Song for Mother's Day" (Tune: "Juanita")

Down in the valley, or upon the mountain height
Where'er the homefires cast their beams by night,
Mothers' hands are helping, mothers' eyes glow clear and bright,
In her heart contentment, tenderness, and light.

When storm clouds threaten, dark the day and night grows long,
And courage falters, making weak the strong,
Then her faith doth strengthen, in her heart a cheering song;
Here no harm can enter, peace and joy belong.

Thy blessing, Father, resting light on Mother mine,
Still she's remembered, may her memory shine
As the jewels of heaven, in a heavenly host benign,
Let her know forever Thy great love divine.

CHORUS:

Mother, dear Mother, sing a song of Mother's love,
Mother, dear Mother, gift of God above.[2]

---

2. "A Song for Mother's Day," by Reverend W. J. Wesenberg, *Sunshine Magazine,* May, 1945. Used by permission of *Sunshine Magazine.*

3RD READER:

A song is born in the heart of a child through a mother's fervent prayer.

> I have worshipped in churches and chapels;
> I've prayed in the busy street;
> I have sought my God and have found him
> Where the waves of his ocean beat;
> I have knelt in the silent forest
> In the shade of some ancient tree;
> But the dearest of all my altars
> Was raised at my mother's knee.
>
> I have listened to God in his temple;
> I've caught his voice in the crowd;
> I have heard him speak when the breakers
> Were booming long and loud;
> Where the winds play soft in the treetops
> My father has talked to me;
> But I never have heard him clearer
> Than I did at my mother's knee.
>
> The things in my life that are worthy
> Were born in my mother's breast,
> And breathed into mine by the majic
> Of the love her life expressed.
> The years that have brought me to manhood
> Have taken her far from me;
> But memory keeps me from straying
> Too far from my mother's knee.
>
> God, make me the man of her vision
> And purge me of selfishness!
> God, keep me true to her standards
> And help me to live to bless!
> God, hallow the holy impress
> Of the days that used to be,
> And keep me a pilgrim forever
> To the shrine at my mother's knee![3]

—JOHN H. STYLES, JR.

TRIO OR QUARTET: "You Taught Me How to Pray"—Helen Jun Marth

---

3. "My Altar" by John H. Styles, Jr. From *Masterpieces of Religious Verse*, edited by James Dalton Morrison. Copyright, 1948, by Harper & Brothers.

LEADER:

As we listen to these songs which our Christian mothers sing, a song of faith, a song of love, and a song of prayer are born in our own hearts. And on this Mother's Day, 19———, as we honor her who gave to us this gift of song, let us bow our heads and lift our hearts in prayer to God who gave this most precious gift to his children:

PRAYER POEM:

> God make my life a lovely light—
> A taper burning fair and tall,
> That casts a radiance warm and bright
> When night and dark shall fall.
>
> God make my life a joyful song—
> A song renewed each day,
> That sorrow may not linger long
> With those who pass my way.
>
> God make my mother's dream come true—
> She dreamed her child would be
> Endowed with strength, yet gentle, too,
> And blessed with gaiety.
>
> God let me to my mother bring
> True honor—let me raise
> My life to her a gallant thing,
> A hymn of living praise![4]

> —ETHEL ARNOLD TILDEN

BENEDICTION HYMN: "I Would Be True"

---

4. "Hymn for a Child on Mother's Day," by Ethel Arnold Tilden. From *Good House-keeping Magazine,* May, 1927. Used by permission of the author.

SERVICE 30

SONGS IN THE NIGHT

(Candlelight or Outdoor Evening Service)

MUSICAL MEDITATION: (violin or quartet) "'Tis So Sweet to Trust in Jesus"

LEADER:

"The Lord will command his lovingkindness in the daytime, and in the night his song shall be with me." "I call to remembrance my song in the night" (Psalms 42:8; 77:6).

Let us call to remembrance a few "songs in the night" which have comforted needy hearts as they walked through the darkness.

STORY:

Let us call to remembrance a song which saved in a night of storm.

"In the midst of a violent storm a ship became helpless owing to a broken rudder. The sound of the breakers on a rocky shore foretold the doom of the vessel. As a forlorn hope the captain put his crew and passengers into boats from which both oars and sails had been lost. The night came down upon them, and a life-saving crew, who had had a glimpse of the ship in its hopeless condition in the darkness, could not find the boats. Discouraged by their useless search, they were nearing a decision to return when, above the roar of the tempest and the sea, they heard a woman's sustained voice singing,

> Sun of my soul, Thou Saviour dear,
> It is not night if Thou be near;
> Oh, may no earth-born cloud arise
> To hide Thee from Thy servant's eyes!

"The song led them to the boats and saved the lives of the ship-wrecked people, who otherwise would have perished."[1]

STORY:

Let us call to remembrance a song which brought courage in a night of captivity.

"While the prisoners of the Union Army during the Civil War were incarcerated in Libby Prison, day after day they saw comrades passing away and their numbers increased by living recruits. One night, about ten o'clock, through the darkness they heard the tramp of feet that soon stopped before the prison door. . . . In the company was a young Baptist minister, whose heart almost fainted when he looked on those cold walls and thought of the suffering inside. Tired and weary, he sat down, put his face in his hands, and wept. Just then a lone voice sang out from an upper window, 'Praise God from whom all blessings flow'; a dozen joined in the second line, more than a score in the third line, and the words, 'Praise Father, Son, and Holy Ghost,' were sung by nearly all the prisoners."

> Praise God, from whom all blessings flow;
> Praise Him, all creatures here below;
> Praise Him above, ye heavenly host;
> Praise Father, Son, and Holy Ghost.

"As the song died away on the still night, the young man arose and sang:

> Prisons would palaces prove,
> If Jesus would dwell with me there.[2]

STORY:

Let us call to remembrance a song which brought light in a night of superstition and fear.

"In India the natives have a superstitious dread of an eclipse of the sun. They fear that the sun is being swallowed by a demon of some sort.

"Once Dr. S. Earl Taylor was in Calcutta during an eclipse of the sun. For days before that event, Dr. Taylor saw the city's streets

1. From *Practical Hymn Studies,* by Edmund S. Lorenz. Copyright, 1937. Used by permission of Fleming H. Revell Company, publishers.
2. Story from *One Hundred and One Hymn Stories,* by Carl F. Price. Copyright, 1923, by Carl F. Price. By permission of Abingdon-Cokesbury Press.

crowded with pilgrims on their way to various sacred places, where they hoped to worship and bathe in the Hooghly River just below the Ganges during the time of the eclipse, expecting thereby to ward off evil. When at last the fateful hour of darkness arrived, hundreds of thousands of natives thronged the sacred waters, terrorized by the eclipse and making a great clamor because they feared that a great power of evil in the form of a snake was about to swallow the sun-god. As Dr. Taylor, looking from the Y. M. C. A. Building, witnessed this terrible evidence of heathenish superstition, he heard a group of native Christians singing in their meeting:

> The whole world was lost in the darkness of sin;
> The Light of the world is Jesus;
> Like sunshine at noon-day His glory shone in;
> The Light of the world is Jesus.
> Come to the Light, 'tis shining for thee;
> Sweetly the Light has dawned upon me;
> Once I was blind, but now I can see;
> The Light of the world is Jesus.

"The effect was thrilling! For India's spiritual darkness is due solely to the eclipse of Jesus, the Light of the world, made by heathenism in the hearts of her benighted millions."[3]

STORY:

Let us call to remembrance a song which afforded protection in a night of physical darkness.

"A blind man was seen crossing the street at a dangerous place in the Bronx, New York City. A friend nearby overheard him singing softly,

> Be not dismayed whate'er betide,
> God will take care of you;
> Beneath His wings of love abide,
> God will take care of you.

> God will take care of you.
> Thro' every day, o'er all the way;
> He will take care of you,
> God will take care of you.

"The friend asked, 'Why are you singing that hymn?' He replied, 'Because I must cross this dangerous street, and maybe one of the

---

3. Ibid.

many wagons might strike me and I might get killed. But the thought came to me that, even if it did occur, my soul would go straight to God. And if He led me across all right, it would be just another evidence of His care of me. So I could not help singing to myself, 'God will take care of you.' Hallelujah!"[4]

STORY:

Let us call to remembrance a song which kindled the light of faith in a night of mental darkness.

"John Henry Newman was returning to France from a visit he had made to Italy. During the voyage on the Mediterranean a dead calm ensued and there were no breezes to move the sails of the vessel. He had been ill and away from friends. As the calm continued there was nothing for the passengers to do but wait and meditate and pray, if so inclined. As a clergyman of England he was perplexed over the state of religion in his country, and lack of spirituality in the Church. . . . So in wonder and perplexity he at length began to write. . . . The hymn was a record of his own personal struggle, his doubt and the uncertainty of his future course. His title for this hymn was 'Light in Darkness,' and it reflects the condition and perplexity of many human hearts."[5]

> Lead, kindly Light, amid th' encircling gloom,
>   Lead Thou me on!
> The night is dark, and I am far from home;
>   Lead Thou me on!
> Keep Thou my feet; I do not ask to see
> The distant scene; one step enough for me.

STORY:

Let us call to remembrance a song which expressed love in a night of hatred and war and blackouts.

"During a Methodist Conference in Atlanta, a surprise air raid alert sounded over the city, and the church where the sessions were held was in darkness for forty minutes. Nearly 1,000 persons waited for the lights to come on and spent the time in song and prayer. In the midst of the blackout, Bishop Arthur J. Moore, who was presiding, spoke quietly, 'Harry, do I hear your voice?' 'Yes, father,' came

---

4. Ibid.
5. From *The Rise and Growth of English Hymnody*, by Harvey B. Marks. Copyright, 1937. Used by permission of Fleming H. Revell Company, publishers.

the reply. 'My son,' said the bishop, 'stand and sing, "My Jesus, I Love Thee.' " And the son obeyed without hesitation.

> My Jesus, I love Thee,
> I know Thou art mine,
> For Thee all the follies of sin I resign;
> My gracious Redeemer,
> My Saviour art Thou;
> If ever I loved Thee, my Jesus 'tis now.

"In this incident we see three things—the father's confidence in his son that he could sing the song without book or light; the son's immediate obedience to the father's command; and the fact that he could not have sung the song if he had not learned it before the emergency.

"Today the world is dark, but when God says, 'My child, stand where you are and sing,' we can do so, if the words are already in our hearts."[6]

PRAYER:

"We thank Thee, O God, that dawn always follows the night, and that in the darkest hours the morning stars sing together."[7] Help us to hear thy "songs in the night" in our own hearts; help us to sing them to others who walk in darkness, that they, too, may know our "Maker, who giveth songs in the night." This we ask in the name of Christ, the Light of the World. Amen.

SUGGESTIONS FOR CARRYING OUT THIS SERVICE:

It is suggested that this service be used as a candlelight or an outdoor evening service. Use as little light as possible (a few candles, or the light of the stars); have each story told by a different storyteller. If the service is used outdoors, the group might be seated in a circle, while the storytellers tell the stories informally.

In the places indicated for the hymns to be sung, all the group may join in the singing of one stanza. These may be led by a song leader who knows the hymns and who is familiar enough with the plan of the service to begin each one at the proper time. Another plan might utilize a soloist or quartet for the hymns instead of using the entire group.

---

6. Written by Mrs. Wallace Rogers. Copyright, 1943, by *The Upper Room*. Nashville, Tennessee, Reprinted by permission.
7. From prayer by E. C. Ford. Copyright, 1943, by *The Upper Room*, Nashville, Tennessee. Reprinted by permission.

SERVICE 31

"LET THERE BE LIGHT"

(A Candlelight Service)

MUSICAL MEDITATION: "The Light of the World Is Jesus"

SCRIPTURE READING:

"In the beginning God created the heaven and the earth. . . . And God said, *Let there be light*: and there was light. And God saw the light, that it was good: and God divided the light from the darkness" (Genesis 1:1, 3-4).

POEM:

> In that far-off dim dawn,
> When chaos reigned, and earth was still
> A formless void in darkness dight,
> The Spirit, brooding o'er the deep,
> Awoke Creation from its sleep
> With that High Call—
> "Let—There—Be—Light!"
> And instant from the womb of night
> Sprang forth the mystic seven-fold beam,
> Ablaze with splendours bright.
> God, in His Wisdom all supreme,
> As His first act made—Light.
>
> So, unto Him give praise!
> Praise without ceasing!—Praise!—
> That in His Wisdom Infinite,
> When making man for His delight,
> Before He dowered him with sight,
> He filled the world with radiance bright,
> Lest, dulled with fear and void of hope,
> With stumbling footsteps he should grope
> Through an eternal night.

To God eternal praise!
Praise without ceasing!—Praise!—
That in His Goodness Infinite
He blessed the world with Light.
Subserve it to His high employ,
And see thou use it right![1]

—JOHN OXENHAM

LEADER:

Men were born upon the earth and walked in this light which their Creator had made, but soon a deeper darkness enveloped them—the darkness of sin—for "men loved darkness rather than light, because their deeds were evil" (John 3:19).

Through the years a few messengers of light came bearing witness that someday God would send another Light into the world—a Light who would dispel this deeper darkness, and give men Light *within* as well as without. Isaiah proclaimed this coming Light in his matchless words, "The people that walked in darkness have seen a great Light: they that dwell in the land of the shadow of death, upon them hath the Light shined" (Isaiah 9:2).

And then, one glorious night, with all God's heavenly lamps alight, and an even greater light blazing forth in the heavens to proclaim his glory, God once more said, "Let there be light," and this greater Light shone forth in a world of darkness and sin.

HYMN: "The Light of the World Is Jesus" (stanza 1)

LEADER:

Life abundant and eternal was to be found in this new Light, given by God to man, for "this life was the Light for men: Amid the darkness the Light shone, but the darkness did not master it" (John 1:4-5—Moffatt).[2] His *message* was one of Light, for Jesus proclaimed, "*I am the light of the world*: he that followeth me shall not walk in darkness, but shall have the light of life" (John 8:12).

HYMN: "The Light of the World Is Jesus" (stanza 2)

---

1. From *The Te Deums and the Sacraments*. Copyright, 1928, by John Oxenham. The Pilgrim Press. Used by permission.
2. *The Bible*, A New Translation, by James Moffatt (New York: Harper and Brothers, 1935). Used by permission.

LEADER:

Today, even as of old, there is deep darkness upon the earth—
the darkness of sin, the darkness of sorrow, the darkness of tragedy
and suffering and need. But none of these darknesses have been able
to master God's Light—the light of the Lord Jesus, which still
shines steadfastly in a world of night. For God is still saying,
"Let there be light" to the blindness of men's minds and the darkness of men's souls, and those who will open eyes long blinded by
darkness may still feel within them the inner glow of his cleansing,
purifying radiance.

HYMN: "The Light of the World Is Jesus" (stanza 3)

LEADER:

How does God say, *"Let there be light"* to those who walk in
darkness today?

1ST CANDLELIGHTER:

God says, *"Let there be light"* to the darkness of men's souls.
Every child of Adam, with his soul darkened by sin, is blind to the
light of the Gospel, for "the god of this world hath blinded the
minds of them which believe not, lest the light of the glorious
gospel of Christ, who is the image of God, should shine unto them"
(2 Corinthians 4:4).

Illumination can come only through "the light of the knowledge
of the glory of God in the face of Jesus Christ" (2 Corinthians
4:6). When this knowledge is found, then may the enlightened
ones sing:

HYMN: "I Heard the Voice of Jesus Say" (stanza 3)

2ND CANDLELIGHTER:

God also says, *"Let there be light"* in the night of sorrow and
suffering. Hear the psalmist as he voices his faith in this Light:
"For thou wilt light my candle: the Lord my God will enlighten
my darkness" (Psalm 18:28).

HYMN: "Lead, Kindly Light" (stanzas 1, 3), or
       "O Love That Wilt Not Let Me Go" (stanza 2)

3RD CANDLELIGHTER:

Another way in which God says, *"Let there be light"* is through his Word. The psalmist proclaims, "Thy Word is a lamp unto my feet, and a light unto my path." "The entrance of thy words giveth light; it giveth understanding unto the simple" (Psalm 119:105, 130).

HYMN: "Thy Word Have I Hid in My Heart" (stanza 1), or
       "O Word of God Incarnate" (stanzas 1, 2, 3)

4TH CANDLELIGHTER:

Finally, God says, *"Ye* are the light of the world," and *"Let there be light"* through *your* shining!

To those of us who have been illumined by Christ's light, he says: "Ye were sometimes darkness, but now are ye light in the Lord: walk as children of light" (Ephesians 5:8). "Shine as lights in the world" (Philippians 2:15). "Let your light so shine before men, that they may see your good works, and glorify your Father which is in heaven" (Matthew 5:16).

And so, the *shining* is committed unto us—the giving of the Light to a sin-darkened world!

His lamp am I . . . to shine where He may say;
And lamps are not for sunny rooms
Nor for the light of day;
But for the dark places of the earth,
Where sin and crime and wrong have birth;
Or for the murky twilight gray
Where wandering souls have gone astray;
Or where the light of faith grows dim,
And souls are groping after Him.

And as sometimes a flame we find,
Clear, shining through the night,
So bright we do not see the lamp,
But only see the light;
So may we shine . . . His love the flame . . .
That men may glorify His name.[3]

—ANNIE JOHNSON FLINT

HYMN: "Let the Lower Lights Be Burning" (all stanzas)

PRAYER (LEADER):

That Christ, the Light of the world, will shine through our lives to light a world in darkness.

HYMN: "Holy Ghost, with Light Divine" (stanzas 1, 4)

SUGGESTIONS FOR CARRYING OUT THIS SERVICE:

This service may be presented as a candlelight service. Have a large picture of Christ placed in the center of the stage, with a large white unlighted candle underneath. Place two smaller unlighted candles on each side of the picture. After the musical meditation period, the leader enters with a lighted candle and begins the story of the creation of Light. As the story of Christ's coming into the world is told, he lights the candle under the picture, thus illuminating the face of the Christ. He then continues his narrative until the question is asked, "How does God say, 'Let there be light' to those who walk in darkness today?"

Each candlelighter then enters in turn and lights one of the candles at the side of the picture, at the same time giving his message of "Light." The parts of leader and candlelighters should be memorized; the songs sung by a concealed soloist, quartet, or choir.

This service may be given in much simpler form if preferred, omitting the candlelighting, and having the hymns sung by the congregation instead of by concealed singers. The service may be varied in a number of ways to fit the occasion and the available equipment.

SERVICE 32

MAKING THE FLAG

(A Patriotic Service)

MUSICAL MEDITATION: "America the Beautiful"

POEM:

Who made the flag? Why, Betsy Ross.
Who else? George Washington helped plan
Our Stars and Stripes. Who else? Who else?
Name me as many as you can!
Why, no one else. Those two
Finished what they set out to do.

Finished? Our flag? Do you forget
Others are making that banner yet?
They made a symbol, and went their way;
It is *we* who are making Our Flag today!
From least to greatest, young and old,
We are helping to fashion its every fold.

That colorful bunting, each flagstaff o'er,
Is only an emblem, nothing more.
But back of that symbol, long years through,
Lies all that a people dream and do.
Hope and longing, courage and skill,
Patience, kindliness, faith, good will;
Humdrum duties from sun to sun,
Vexations conquered, victories won.
And a forward look, when efforts lag:
These are the stuff that makes Our Flag!
For the loveliest banner, near or far,
Is only whatever its citizens are.[1]

---

1. "Who Made the Flag?" by Frances Crosby Hamlet. From *Sunshine Magazine*, July 1943. Used by permission of *Sunshine Magazine*.

LEADER:

"Our flag symbolizes for us all the beauty and charm and high ideals of our homeland.

"Its red stands for courage, moral as well as physical."[2]

> Courage, the highest gift, that scorns to bend
> To mean devices for a sordid end.
> Courage—an independent spark from heaven's bright throne.
> By which the soul stands raised, triumphant, high, alone.
> Great in itself, not praises of the crowd,
> Above all vice, it stoops not to be proud.
> Courage, the mighty attribute of powers above,
> By which those great in war are great in love.
> The spring of all brave acts is stated here,
> As falsehoods draw their sordid birth from fear.

> —FARQUHAR

HYMN: "Dare to Be Brave, Dare to Be True" (stanzas 1, 3)

LEADER:

The white of our flag "is symbolic of purity, which cannot flourish amidst hate and fear and prejudice."*

> He serves his country best
> Who lives pure life and doeth righteous deed,
> And walks straight paths however others stray,
> And leaves his sons, as uttermost bequest,
> A stainless record which all men may read;
>   This is the better way.
> No drop but serves the slowly lifting tide;
> No dew but has an errand to some flower;
> No smallest star but sheds some helpful ray,
> And man by man, each helping all the rest,
> Make the firm bulwark of the country's power;
>   There is no better way.

> —SUSAN COOLIDGE

HYMN: "Rise Up, O Men of God" (all stanzas)

LEADER:

The blue of our flag "stands for truth and loyalty."*

---

2. These statements and those starred (*) are by Jesse H. Holmes.

STORY:

"My little son and I stood on the village square of my old home town. It was an exhilarating Sunday morning.

" 'There,' said I, as I pointed to a dilapidated church house, 'there is where my father used to go to church, when he was a boy. Twice each Sunday father used to ring that church bell, and when the people heard the bell, they all came to church to worship their God.'

"I had scarcely ceased speaking when my son looked up and said, 'Daddy, why don't they ring the bell now?'

"I stood there looking at the silent bell. The leaning steeple seemed to come closer—I was lost in the memories of the past. There was a tug at my hand, and the child's voice said again, 'Daddy, why don't they ring the bell now?' And with that voice I seemed to hear the voices of children from all around the country-side—poor, ragged, sad, wicked children with no place to go to learn of life. All these stretched out their hands, pleading, 'Why don't they ring the bell now?' Sick children called to me in weak and faint voices. Lonely ones looked at me pitifully. In many voices they all cried, 'Why don't they ring the bell now?'

"I looked about me that Sunday morning. I saw one man mowing his lawn. Across the street a family was putting a picnic-lunch into the car. Farther down, another man sat on the porch yawning. In his driveway, another was polishing his new car. Still another was pruning his hedge. On a nearby stone steps, three children sat absorbing the comic section of a big Sunday newspaper.

" 'Is this America?' I thought. 'Was this what our forefathers did to make America great?' Why were these people not in church? If our fathers in their day could not live without the church, can we live without it in this day of new and greater sin? With the passing of our fathers, will the church also pass?

"I lifted my voice with the voice of my son, and cried, 'Why don't they ring the bell now?' "[3]

---

3. From *Sunshine Magazine*, September, 1943. Used by permission.

HYMN: "O Jesus, Thou Art Standing" (all stanzas), or
"God of Our Fathers, Known of Old" (all stanzas), or
"Loyalty to Christ" (stanzas 1, 2, 4)

LEADER:

"Let us then pledge allegiance to our flag, with a renewed sense of being loyal every day of our lives.

"Let us see that everyone in this country gets an equal opportunity to enjoy its privileges."*

SALUTE TO THE AMERICAN FLAG:

"I pledge allegiance to the flag of the United States of America and to the Republic for which it stands: one Nation, indivisible, with liberty and justice for all."

HYMN: "America" (stanzas 1, 4)

LEADER: "It's Just a Piece of Cloth."

"That is all it is—just a piece of cloth. But when a little breeze comes along, it stirs and comes to life, and flutters and snaps in the wind, all red and white and blue! And then you realize that no other piece of cloth could be like it.

"It has your whole life wrapped up in it: the meals you eat; the time you spend with your family; the kind of things your boy and girl learn at school; the strange and wonderful thoughts you get in church on Sunday.

"Those stars in it—they make you feel just as free as the stars in the wide, deep night. And those stripes—they are bars of blood to any dictator who would try to change this way of life.

"Just a piece of cloth, that is all—until you put your soul into it, and give it meaning. Then it is a symbol of liberty, and decency, and fair-dealing for everyone. It is just a piece of cloth until we breathe life into it; until we make it stand for everything we believe in, and refuse to live without!"[4]—Victory Message in *Westinghouse Magazine*.

If it were given voice and could speak to us today, I think that this would be its message:

---

4. From *Sunshine Magazine*, June, 1944. Used by permission.

I am whatever you make me, nothing more.
I swing before your eyes as a bright gleam of color,
A symbol of yourself,
A pictured suggestion of that big thing
Which makes this nation.
My stars and my stripes are your dream and your labors.
They are bright with cheer,
Brilliant with courage, firm with faith,
Because you have made them so out of your hearts.
We are all making the flag.

—FRANKLIN K. LANE

PRAYER:

"God of the nations, Father of all, we would worship thee in the spirit of true patriotism; with reverence to thy holy name, honor and glory to all that thy spirit, working in thy world, has created, and love shown in deeds of courage and true valor.

"We praise thee for brave men and courageous deeds which have brought our country to its place of leadership among the nations. Help us to prize and guard the noble heritage which is ours in the heroic achievement of liberty and law.

"Forgive us for any thought or deed which might endanger the freedom wrought for us by our forefathers. Give truth to our words, and courage to our deeds as we make patriotism beautiful with loyalty and devotion. Amen."

—AUTHOR UNKNOWN

HYMN: "Faith of Our Fathers" (all stanzas), or
      "The Star-Spangled Banner" (stanzas 1, 4)

SUGGESTIONS FOR CARRYING OUT THIS SERVICE:

As a visual aid to this service, a flannelgraph of an American flag could be made by the leader as the service progresses. This can be done by setting up a background for the flag and covering it with flannel or by using a flannelgraph board if one is available. Prepare red and white stripes, and a field of blue with white stars. On the back of each of these, paste a piece of flannel the same size. As the red of the flag is featured in the service, have someone place the red stripes in place on the flannel background. Do the same when the white stripes and the field of blue are mentioned. Thus, by the time the salute to the American flag is to be given, an American flag has been visibly made and is ready for the salute, which should be given by the entire group.

If the above plan is not practicable, a large American flag can be placed before the group at the beginning of the service to serve the same purpose.

SERVICE 33

"MY COVENANT"

(Service based on B. S. U. pamphlet, "My Covenant")

MUSICAL MEDITATION: (Organ or piano) "Speak to My Heart"

LEADER: Brief explanation of "My Covenant"

OPENING MEDITATION (reader):

(Organ or piano begins to play "Tread Softly" as reading begins and continues through directed prayer.)

> I had walked life's way with an easy tread,
> Had followed where comforts and pleasures led;
> Until one day, in a quiet place,
> I met the Master face to face.
>
> With station and rank and wealth for my goal,
> Much thought for my body, but none for my soul,
> I had entered to win in life's mad race
> When I met the Master face to face.
>
> I met Him and knew Him, and blushed to see
> That His eyes, full of sorrow, were fixed on me;
> And I faltered and fell at His feet that day,
> While my castles melted and vanished away.
>
> Melted and vanished, and in their place
> Naught else did I see but the Master's face,
> And I cried aloud, "Oh, make me meet
> To follow the steps of Thy wounded feet."
>
> My thoughts are now for the souls of men.
> I have lost my life to find it again,
> E'er since one day, in a quiet place,
> I met the Master face to face.
>
> —ANONYMOUS

DIRECTED PRAYER (leader):

Let us pray:
That in this quiet place of meditation we, too, may meet the Master face to face.

(Pause for silent prayer.)

That we may feel His presence in this quiet hour, for "closer is He than breathing, and nearer than hands and feet" (Tennyson)

(Pause for silent prayer.)

That, in the stillness, we may hear His still, small Voice, calling us to be mastered by the Master in every realm of our lives.

(Pause for silent prayer.)

That we may look into the Master's face and say in all sincerity and truth:

> In full and glad surrender we give ourselves to thee,
> Thine utterly and only and evermore to be!
> O Son of God, who lovest us, we will be thine alone,
> And all we are and all we have shall henceforth be thine own.

> —FRANCES RIDLEY HAVERGAL

SOLO OR QUARTET: "Tread Softly" (to be sung as closing prayer of meditation period)

ORGAN OR PIANO: "O Happy Day" (Begin to play as reader begins reading of Covenant; continue through reading on *Salvation*.)

READER: (reading Covenant)

"Earnestly desiring to grow into greater usefulness and spiritual power as a CHRISTIAN and as a CHURCH MEMBER, I solemnly but joyously engage myself in this holy covenant between myself and my Lord.

(Pause as music continues)

"In humility and penitence I recall or make certain my experience of regeneration, or conversion, by and through which definite act of my will I became a child of God, a follower of Jesus Christ, and upon which alone I am definitely depending for the salvation of my soul throughout time and eternity."

SOLO OR QUARTET: "O Happy Day" (stanza 1)

ORGAN OR PIANO: "I Surrender All," or "Nothing Between"
(Play through reading of *Worldliness Out.*)

READER:

"Believing that worldliness and spirituality are antitheses; that
the Scriptures teach and the lives of greatest Christians illustrate
that constant restraint in affairs social and otherwise is necessary to
spiritual growth, I gladly covenant between myself and my Lord
that I will refrain from all indulgences about which I have any
doubt in reason or conscience. 'Whether therefore ye eat, or drink,
or whatsoever ye do, do all to the glory of God' " (1 Corinthians
10:31).

SOLO OR QUARTET: "I Surrender All" (stanza 2), or
"Nothing Between" (stanza 2)

ORGAN OR PIANO: "Thy Word Have I Hid in My Heart," or "Break
Thou the Bread of Life"
(Play through reading of *Bible Study.*)

READER:

"Believing definitely that the Holy Scripture is the food upon
which the soul and the spirit of a Christian must feed for life and
growth, I gladly covenant between myself and my Lord that I will
spend habitually [*a certain portion of time*] each day—if possible
at the same time each day—in private reading and study of God's
Word."

SOLO OR QUARTET: "Thy Word Have I Hid in My Heart" (stanza
1), or "Break Thou the Bread of Life" (stanza 1)

ORGAN OR PIANO: "Did You Think to Pray?" or "Sweet Hour of
Prayer"
(Play through reading of *Prayer and Meditation.*)

READER:

"Believing that spiritual power and growth are impossible aside
from prayer, I gladly covenant with myself and my Lord as follows:

"(1) I will spend each day, as nearly as possible at the same time and place—except when providentially prevented—at least [*a designated portion of time*] in private meditation and prayer;

"(2) Claiming the promise of Matthew 18:19, 'That if two of you shall agree on earth as touching any thing that they shall ask, it shall be done for them of my Father which is in heaven,' I will, while in college, seek to have one or more Prayer-mates with whom I shall pray regularly for the will of God to be done in my life, on my campus, and in the world."

SOLO OR QUARTET: "Did You Think to Pray?" (stanza 1), or
"Sweet Hour of Prayer" (stanza 1)

ORGAN OR PIANO: "I Love Thy Kingdom, Lord"

(Play through reading of *Church Loyalty*)

READER:

"Believing that Christ established one and only one earthly institution to which he committed the work of extending his kingdom, and believing also that the world's greatest Christian characters have usually been loyal to that institution, I gladly covenant that I will be conscientiously loyal to my (local) church."

SOLO OR QUARTET: "I Love Thy Kingdom, Lord" (stanzas 2, 3)

ORGAN OR PIANO: "O Day of Rest and Gladness"

(Play through reading of *Sabbath Observance*.)

READER:

"Believing that God had a purpose in establishing one day in seven to be holy unto him, that most great Christian characters of ancient and modern times have observed that day as holy unto the Lord, and that a strict observance of the day as holy will benefit me physically, mentally and spiritually, I gladly covenant with myself and my Lord that I will 'Remember the Sabbath day to keep it holy.' "

SOLO OR QUARTET: "O Day of Rest and Gladness" (stanza 1)

ORGAN OR PIANO: "Take My Life and Let It Be," or "Something for Thee"

(Play through reading of *Christian Ownership*.)

READER:

"Believing the scriptural teaching that God is owner and I am his steward, and seeking to save myself from the sin of covetousness, I gladly covenant with myself and my Lord that I will live out the principle of stewardship of talents, time, and service, and, so far as my means go, I will practice the giving of the tithe."

SOLO OR QUARTET: "Take My Life and Let It Be" (stanzas 1, 3), or "Something for Thee" (stanza 1)

ORGAN OR PIANO: "Lord, Lay Some Soul Upon My Heart," or "O Master, Let Me Walk with Thee"

(Play through reading of *Christian Witnessing*.)

READER:

"Believing that the highest human service to my fellow man and the highest quality of service to my Lord is that of leading an unsaved, unregenerate person to the Saviour, and believing that the world's most powerful Christians have been active personal soul-winners, I gladly covenant with myself and my Lord that I will conscientiously seek out and try to win lost souls to Christ."

SOLO OR QUARTET: "Lord, Lay Some Soul Upon My Heart" (stanza 1), or
"O Master, Let Me Walk with Thee" (stanzas 1, 2)

ORGAN OR PIANO: "All on the Altar, Dear Jesus"

(Play through conclusion of Covenant and continue playing through period of silent prayer.)

READER:

"Believing that a definite commitment of myself will help me in the keeping of this covenant, I formally sign it at the time, place, and date here indicated and shall keep it in my own possession. This covenant is secret, personal, and holy."

Closing Meditation (leader):

Take thou our minds, dear Lord, we humbly pray;
Give us the mind of Christ each passing day;
Teach us to know the truth that sets us free;
Grant us in all our thoughts to honor thee.

Take thou our hearts, O Christ, they are thine own;
Come thou within our souls and claim thy throne;
Help us to shed abroad thy deathless love;
Use us to make the earth like heaven above.

Take thou our wills, Most High! hold thou full sway;
Have in our inmost souls thy perfect way;
Guard thou each sacred hour from selfish ease;
Guide thou our ordered lives as thou dost please.

Take thou ourselves, O Lord, heart, mind, and will;
Through our surrendered souls thy plans fulfill.
We yield ourselves to thee—time, talents, all;
We hear, and henceforth heed, thy sovereign call.[1]

—William H. Foulkes

Silent Prayer of Consecration

Solo or Quartet: "All on the Altar, Dear Jesus"

Suggestions for Carrying Out This Service:

This service may be used to introduce "My Covenant" of the Master's Minority Movement to a group of college students. It is intended that the service be one of quiet meditation and prayer, in which the students earnestly consider the claims of Christ upon their lives as presented in the eight points of the "Covenant." They are then to take them into some quiet place alone with God and sign the covenant in secret, as the Spirit leads them.

Copies of the Baptist Student Union pamphlet, "My Covenant," are issued free by the Department of Student Work, Sunday School Board of the Southern Baptist Convention, Nashville, Tennessee. These may be secured and placed in the hands of every young person present. Have them given out as the young people enter the place of worship; they should carry them to their seats and study them during the opening musical meditation period. Before

---

1. Copyright, 1918, by Calvin W. Laufer. Used by permission of Edward B. Laufer.

the worship service begins, the leader may explain briefly the meaning and purpose of the Master's Minority Covenant.

The reader of the covenant and the musicians should be concealed. A continuous musical background should be maintained throughout. This will require careful rehearsing on the part of accompanist, reader, and singers in order to assure a smooth, effective presentation of the service.

Some worship leaders may find the following slightly altered plan preferable to the one suggested. Instead of having the covenant read by a reader, the members of the group may be instructed to read each section of the covenant silently, meditating upon it as the musical background is played and sung. Preceding each section of the covenant, the leader should indicate the section to be considered, introducing each with a few words, such as, "Let us meditate upon the joyous fact of our salvation," "Let us consider God's claims upon us for church loyalty," etc. Following this, the organist or pianist may play the hymn indicated on the program while the group reads and meditates upon the portion of the covenant, after which the soloist or quartet may sing the hymn indicated.

SERVICE 34

"WHAT HAST THOU GIVEN FOR ME?"

(A Missionary Service)

MUSICAL MEDITATION: "I Gave My Life for Thee"
(played softly by piano or organ, or by violin and piano)

The Call

SCRIPTURE READING:

"And a vision appeared to Paul in the night; There stood a man of Macedonia, and prayed him, saying, Come over into Macedonia, and help us. And after he had seen the vision, immediately we endeavoured to go into Macedonia, assuredly gathering that the Lord had called us for to preach the gospel unto them" (Acts 16:9-10).

DUET: "How Long Must We Wait?" (stanza 1)

(Pianist continues playing this hymn softly as the following poem is read):

POEM:

Is it nothing to you, all ye that pass by,
That hosts of my children are hungry for bread,
While you at the tables of plenty are fed?
How can you be deaf to their cry?

Is it nothing to you, all ye that pass by,
That millions in darkness of soul cry for light,
While you, whom Christ's love saved from similar plight,
Have knowledge to answer that cry?

Is it nothing to you, all ye that pass by,
That Christ, the World-Saviour, hath trusted in you
As He loved, to love; as He did, to do?
Would you His commission deny?

Is it nothing to you, all ye that pass by,
O, waken from half-hearted prayer and desire;
Be filled with His Spirit, aflame with His fire!
Only then shall His kingdom draw nigh.

—CATHERINE CULLEN

DUET: "How Long Must We Wait?" (stanza 3)

Our Responsibility

SCRIPTURE READING:

"Whosoever shall call upon the name of the Lord shall be saved.
How then shall they call on him in whom they have not believed?
and how shall they believe in him of whom they have not heard?
and how shall they hear without a preacher? and how shall they
preach, except they be sent?" (Romans 10:13-15).

HYMN: "We've a Story to Tell to the Nations" (stanza 1)
(Music of this hymn continues through reading of following
poem):

POEM:

I know a soul that is steeped in sin,
That no man's art can cure;
But I know a Name, a Name, a Name
That can make that soul all pure.

I know a life that is lost to God,
Bound down by the things of earth;
But I know a Name, a Name, a Name
That can bring that soul new birth.

I know of lands that are sunk in shame,
Of hearts that faint and tire;
But I know a Name, a Name, a Name
That can set those lands on fire.

Its sound is a brand, its letters flame
Like glowing tongues of fire.
I know a Name, a Name, a Name
That will set those lands on fire.

—AUTHOR UNKNOWN

Hymn: "We've a Story to Tell to the Nations" (stanza 4)

Our Response

(1) *In Praying*

Scripture Reading:

Jesus said, "The harvest truly is plenteous, but the labourers are few; *Pray ye* therefore the Lord of the harvest, that he will send forth labourers into his harvest" (Matthew 9:37-38).

Leader:

Let us bow our heads for a period of silent meditation and prayer.

Quartet: "O God, We Pray for All Mankind" (stanza 1)
(Tune: "Ortonville")

> O God, we pray for all mankind,
> The nations far astray;
> We plead that all Thy grace may find,
> In this Thy gracious day,
> In this Thy gracious day.

(Music of this hymn continues through reading of poem)

Poem:

> The weary ones had rest, the sick had joy that day
>   And wondered how—
> The ploughman singing at his work had prayed:
>   "God help them now."
>
> Alone in foreign lands, they wondered how
>   Their feeble words had power—
> At home the Christians, two or three, had met
>   To pray an hour.
>
> So we are always wondering, wondering long,
>   Because we do not see
> Some one, unknown, perhaps, and far away,
>   On bended knee.

                                          —Anonymous

Quartet: "O God, We Pray for All Mankind" (stanza 3)

> With humble plea on Thee we call
> For nations in distress;
> Of one hast thou not made us all?
> O God, our kindred bless!
> O God, our kindred bless!

(This should be used as a prayer hymn, with congregation bowed in silent prayer as it is sung. After the singing of the third stanza, the pianist may play it through once more, or the quartet may hum it through softly, as the period of silent prayer is continued. The quartet then sings the fourth stanza, adding "Amen" to conclude the period of silent prayer.)

Stanza 4:

> Help all the nations, near and far,
> Awake, Thy glory see;
> Behold the bright and morning star,
> The Christ of Calvary.
> The Christ of Calvary. Amen.

—HOWARD J. CONOVER

(2) *In Giving*

SCRIPTURE READING:

"Honour the Lord with thy substance, and with the first fruits of all thine increase" (Proverbs 3:9).

"Bring ye all the tithes into the storehouse, that there may be meat in mine house, and prove me now herewith, saith the Lord of hosts, if I will not open you the windows of heaven, and pour you out a blessing, that there shall not be room enough to receive it" (Malachi 3:10).

"For ye know the grace of our Lord Jesus Christ, that, though he was rich, yet for your sakes he became poor, that ye through his poverty might be rich" (2 Corinthians 8:9).

Therefore, "Upon the first day of the week let every one of you lay by him in store, as God hath prospered him" (1 Corinthians 16:2).

"Every man according as he purposeth in his heart, so let him give; not grudgingly, or of necessity; for God loveth a cheerful giver" (2 Corinthians 9:7).

Let us "remember the words of the Lord Jesus, how he said, It is more blessed to give than to receive" (Acts 20:35).

HYMN: "I Gave My Life for Thee" (stanza 1)

(Music of this hymn continues while offering is being taken.)

MISSIONARY OFFERING

HYMN: "I Gave My Life for Thee" (stanza 4)

(3) *In Going*

SCRIPTURE READING:

"Go ye therefore, and teach all nations, baptizing them in the name of the Father, and of the Son, and of the Holy Ghost: teaching them to observe all things whatsoever I have commanded you: and, lo, I am with you alway, even unto the end of the world" (Matthew 28:19-20).

SOLO: "Hark, the Voice of Jesus Calling" (stanza 1)

(Music continues through reading)

POEM:

Read

> There's only one way that the lost world can know
>   That Jesus for sinners has died;
> To tell the glad story He's bidden us go,
>   And no other way doth provide.
>
> If Christ's first disciples had silently gone,
>   And been to their great trust untrue,
> His plan of salvation we could not have known—
>   His mercy for me and for you.
>
> He's counting on us the story to tell,
>   His plan of redemption to man;
> He's counting on me, He's counting on you,
>   The Master has no other plan.

—MRS. C. H. MORRIS

SOLO: "Hark, the Voice of Jesus Calling" (stanza 4)

PRAYER

SUGGESTIONS FOR CARRYING OUT THIS SERVICE:

It is suggested that the outline of this service be placed upon a blackboard or in some way be visibly presented to the group participating. The songs to be used by the congregation may be listed with this outline:

"WHAT HAST THOU GIVEN FOR ME?"

Period of Meditation

1. The Call
2. Our Responsibility
3. Our Response
    (1) In Praying
    (2) In Giving
    (3) In Going

If a missionary offering is to be taken, announce it before the service begins so that no further announcement in the service will be necessary.

The message of this service will be much more effective if the ones participating in the special numbers (solo, duet, quartet) be stationed in some concealed place.

SERVICE 35

"ENTER INTO HIS GATES WITH THANKSGIVING"

(Thanksgiving and Praise Service)

CALL TO WORSHIP:
"It is a good thing to give thanks unto the Lord, and to sing praises unto thy name, O most High" (Psalm 92:1).

HYMN: "Praise God from Whom All Blessings Flow" (Doxology)

UNISON SCRIPTURE READING WITH HYMNS:

GROUP: "O come, let us sing unto the Lord: let us make a joyful noise to the rock of our salvation" (Psalm 95:1).

HYMN: "Come, Thou Fount of Every Blessing"

GROUP: "Let us come before his presence with thanksgiving, and make a joyful noise unto him with psalms. For the Lord is a great God, and a great King above all gods" (Psalm 95:2-3).

HYMN: "Come, Thou Almighty King"

GROUP: "In his hand are the deep places of the earth: the strength of the hills is his also. The sea is his, and he made it: and his hands formed the dry land" (Psalm 95:4-5).

HYMN: "This Is My Father's World," or
"For the Beauty of the Earth"

GROUP: "O come, let us worship and bow down: let us kneel before the Lord our maker" (Psalm 95:6).

Hymn: "All Hail the Power," or
     "O Worship the King"

Group: "Make a joyful noise unto the Lord, all ye lands. Serve
the Lord with gladness: come before his presence with
singing" (Psalm 100:1-2).

Hymn: "O for a Thousand Tongues to Sing," or
     "Serve the Lord with Gladness"

Group: "Know ye that the Lord he is God: it is he that hath made
us, and not we ourselves; we are his people, and the sheep
of his pasture" (Psalm 100:3).

Hymn: "The Lord Is My Shepherd"

Group: "Enter into his gates with thanksgiving, and into his courts
with praise: be thankful unto him, and bless his name"
(Psalm 100:4).

Hymn: "Rejoice, Ye Pure in Heart"

Group: "For the Lord is good; his mercy is everlasting; and his
truth endureth to all generations" (Psalm 100:5).

Hymn: "Praise Him! Praise Him!"

Poem (to be read responsively):

Leader:
         Praise ye the Father, praise the Lord most holy,
         Who cheers the contrite, girds with strength the weak;

Group:
         Praise Him who will with glory crown the lowly,
         And with salvation beautify the meek.

Leader:
         Praise ye the Lord, for all His loving kindness,
         And all the tender mercy He hath shown;

Group:
         Praise Him who pardons all our sin and blindness,
         And calls us sons, and takes us for His own.

LEADER:

> Praise ye the Father, source of every blessing,
> Before His gifts earth's richest boons are dim.

GROUP:

> Resting in Him, His peace and joy possessing,
> All things are ours, for we have all in Him.

LEADER:

> Praise ye the Father, God the Lord who gave us,
> With full and perfect love, His only Son;

GROUP:

> Praise ye the Son who died Himself to save us;
> Praise ye the Spirit, praise the Three in One.
> —M. COCKBURN-CAMPBELL

BENEDICTION HYMN: "Saviour, Again to Thy Dear Name We Raise" (stanza 1)

SUGGESTIONS FOR CARRYING OUT THIS SERVICE:

This service will be most effective if a copy of the Scripture and hymn selections and the praise poem is placed in the hands of each of the group, and all participate in the Scripture reading and in the singing of the hymns together. As many stanzas of the hymns may be used as time allows.

For the latter part of this service, the old setting of the one hundredth Psalm, "All People That on Earth Do Dwell," to the tune of the Doxology (Old Hundred), may be used instead of the suggested hymns, if desired. This hymn setting of the one hundredth Psalm is especially fitting to be used at the Thanksgiving season, as it was sung in this setting in the early American churches by the Pilgrim Fathers.

SERVICE 36

"WE HAVE SEEN HIS STAR"[1]

(A Carol Service)

READER:

It was a typical Christmas Eve. The mystic spell of the night was upon me as I swept my unfinished work into the desk, slipped into a heavy coat, and went out onto my upper porch, among the treetops. "I will look for His star!" I said.

The night was mild, but with the nip of frost in the air, a feathery snow on the mountains. Oh, the white stillness of them! As if they, too, were holding their breath to listen. As if their peaks had pierced the veil between heaven and earth, and could see the wondering, waiting angels. I sank down gratefully, to absorb the peace of the heavens. "This," said a rapt, small voice in my heart, "is the night He will come!" And in the bare branches of the tree tops there was the soft breeze that old-time carolers believed was the silent singing of angels.

Suddenly there shone a new light across the street, then several. They gleamed through the stained glass window of the little frame community church, making a path of glory in the snow. Evidently the union choir practice of carols was to be here this year. Cheery voices came up to me, the stamping of feet on the worn steps, then the notes of the organ and a deep, powerful voice sending forth that joyously stirring Christmas call:

> "O come, all ye faithful,
> Joyful and triumphant,
> O come ye, O come ye to Bethlehem."

What *is* there about these grand old hymns that they can, with almost a single chord, bridge the centuries and make the past as

---

1. Adapted from "We Have Seen His Star," by Beatrice Plumb, *Christian Herald*, December, 1933. Used by permission of *Christian Herald*.

yesterday? With a line or two recreate the stirring days that produced them, before your very eyes?

See the holy men of the thirteenth century chanting it, to its earlier music, as they move slowly along in stately procession to the sanctuary where they are to meet for the Christmas morning service. Is the lowly friar, Bonaventura, the author? Or did he merely translate from a still earlier manuscript? But whether seven hundred years old or a thousand, the grand old hymn, in one form or another, has called untold multitudes to follow the Star.

Its present tune? Well, that was made for a king. By one Marco, a musician born in Lisbon in 1763, who eventually became chapel master to the King of Portugal. It was his duty now, instead of composing grand opera, to train the "Children of the Chapel Royal"—boy singers in the king's own choir. And he composed this regal tune with its rallying, manly ring as an offertory piece to be played while people brought their offerings to the altar.

A tune made for a king! But somehow it managed to escape the palace and was next heard in the Portuguese Chapel, London, and soon that ringing offertory tune was accompanying a star-led world as it went forward, singing, to lay its gifts at the feet of the manger-cradled Babe of Bethlehem.

CAROL: "O Come, All Ye Faithful"

READER:

There! The grand harmony of Mark, the Portuguese, had stopped. Now they were ready to begin in earnest, and soon the voices of the full chorus swept up to me.

> "Hark! The herald angels sing
> Glory to the new-born King!"

Ah, that was Charles Wesley's beautiful Christmas gift to the world! And that gloriously exultant tune that seems to mount up and up as if to meet the distant singing of an unseen heavenly host was written by a Jew. For it was taken from the great Felix Mendelssohn's cantata, *Gott Ist Licht*. The same Mendelssohn who rose from an open Bible to devote nine years of inspired labor to his wonderful oratorio of *Elijah*. Who poured his very life into it; for within a year of its completion he said, "I can not play. . . . I have no strength," and died. And not yet forty!

CAROL: "Hark, the Herald Angels Sing"

READER:

But—listen! The boy soloist was singing—in that hushed tone that somehow held in it all that shone in his eyes of things we older folk could neither see nor hear:

> O little town of Bethlehem!
>   How still we see thee lie;
> Above thy deep and dreamless sleep
>   The silent stars go by;
> Yet in thy dark streets shineth
>   The everlasting Light;
> The hopes and fears of all the years
>   Are met in thee tonight.

A memory set to a dream-tune! Written by a young clergyman who three years before had kept tryst in the very field where tradition says the shepherds saw the Star. It was at the Christmas season, and he wrote, "The shepherds were still keeping watch over their flocks or leading them home to the fold."

There in the brooding silence he, too, must have seen the Star; for if ever a man's whole life was lived in the light of it, it was his. For this was young Phillips Brooks, who was to become "Brooks, the beloved" of Boston, spiritual guide to a nation; and finally, the Bishop of Massachusetts.

But it was not the eloquent Bishop I heard in the sweet notes that were pouring from the little choir boy's throat as naturally as from a bird's. Here was the divine glow of consecrated youth. For even the tune was written by a young man—Lewis Henry Redner, Brooks' junior by several years. He was church organist and Sunday school superintendent, and the two were close friends. Phillips Brooks asked this exceedingly busy young man to write a tune for his new Bethlehem hymn, so that the children could sing it the following Sunday.

He readily consented, but during the week a thousand extra Christmas duties pressed in on him, so that Saturday night found him too utterly worn out with much serving to compose a single bar. Mentally and physically exhausted, he fell into bed, his last wearied, worried thought of the one thing he had not done—the one thing he had really wanted to do.

In the middle of the night he was awakened by what he calls "an angel strain." He listened. It came again. Note by note, a sweet, slow melody, as tranquil as little Bethlehem sleeping beneath the silent stars. Joyously he arose to record it; and so we have another lovely, heaven-sent thing to lay at the feet of the Bethlehem Babe.

CAROL: "O Little Town of Bethlehem"

READER:

But now a guitar hushed us into a deep silence, and with it was the clear voice of the little chorister again, singing one of the loveliest of German carols:

> Silent night, Holy night!
> All is calm, all is bright,
> Round yon Virgin Mother and Child,
> Holy Infant, so tender and mild,
> Sleep in heavenly peace,
> Sleep in heavenly peace.

Did they know it had been first played on a guitar because the church organ was out of order? And after that, had been carried abroad in the land by a company of strolling Tyrol minstrels who appropriated it for their repertoire, thus becoming the "mystery carol"? Whose was it? One Joseph had written the words, they shrugged, and one Franz, the tune. That was all the strolling singers knew. Instantly it was credited to the great composer, Franz Joseph Haydn.

But no! Investigation found the poem had been written by Joseph Mohr, assistant priest in Oberndorf, Germany, the tune composed by Franz Gruber, a humble schoolmaster. They themselves sang it in the little church on Christmas Eve, 1818, to the accompaniment of a guitar. How little they guessed it was destined to tune the hushed souls of millions to the spiritual key of Christmas!

CAROL: "Silent Night, Holy Night"

READER:

The choir across the street was now apparently getting ready to disband. They were standing, in coats and mufflers, on the porch. And they hadn't sung "Joy to the World!" I was terribly disappointed.

But, hark! What was that? The bells! Suddenly I was on my feet. So were all the muffled figures on the porches. Late as that? I marveled. *That's* what the choir had waited for. Midnight! In the white stillness we stood there, counting the chimes to Christmas! As the last one rose exultantly to the mountaintops, my longed-for hymn rose triumphantly after it, and I knew that I, too, had seen His Star!

CAROL: "Joy to the World"

For other services appropriate for the Christmas season, see "Here We Come A-Caroling" and "Led By a Star" (Part Three).

PART III

SERVICES IN SONG

FOR

CHOIR USE

MUSIC IN A CHURCH

Softly—slowly the music begins,
The organ tones weaving accompaniment to the harmony
     of many voices.
Then gradually the tempo increases;
More swiftly moves the melody—faster and faster with
     a definite purpose.
The sounds grow louder,
Penetrating every nook and corner
'Til the whole room is filled with the beautiful music,
     and vibrates with the intenseness of it.
On and on it goes,
Rising to a final great climax—
A climax which when attained, is the completion of a work
     of God's own hand,
Reaching into the depths of the human soul.

—MARY ELLEN INMAN

Used by permission of the author and the National Poetry Association.

SERVICE 37

THE LIFE OF CHRIST IN SONG

CONGREGATIONAL HYMN: "Thou Didst Leave Thy Throne"

READER: Hear the words of the prophet Isaiah as he foretold the coming of the promised Messiah: Isaiah 11:1-2; 7:14.

YOUTH CHOIR: "O Come, O Come, Emmanuel"—Gregorian melody, 8th century

READER: Galatians 4:4-5; Luke 2:8-11

SOPRANO SOLO, QUARTET OR CHOIR: "O Holy Night"—Adam

READER: Isaiah 9:2, 6

CONGREGATIONAL HYMN: "O Come, All Ye Faithful"

READER: Acts 10:38; Matthew 15:29-31

SOLO OR YOUTH CHOIR: "The Stranger of Galilee"—Mrs. C. H. Morris

READER: Isaiah 53:10a; Luke 22:39-44

YOUTH CHOIR: "Into the Woods My Master Went"—George B. Nevin, or
"Into the Woods My Master Went"—Peter C. Lutkin

READER: John 19:16-18; Isaiah 53:4-6

MALE QUARTET: "Were You There?"—Negro Spiritual

READER: Matthew 28:1-6

CONGREGATIONAL HYMN: "Christ the Lord Is Risen Today"

READER: Philippians 2:9-11

YOUTH CHOIR: "Crusader's Hymn" (Beautiful Saviour)—Melody of 12th century, arr. by Wick

YOUTH CHOIR: "The Lord Bless You and Keep You"—Peter C. Lutkin

SERVICE 38

THE WAY OF THE CROSS

The Choice of the Way

READING (by Choral Speaking Choir):
"Then said Jesus unto his disciples, If any man will come after me, let him deny himself, and take up his cross, and follow me. For whosoever will save his life shall lose it: and whosoever will lose his life for my sake shall find it" (Matthew 16:24-25).

CHOIR: Medley of Hymns
    "Take Up Thy Cross"
        Tenors and altos—stanza 1
        Tenor solo—first phrase of refrain (altos hum)
        Tenors and altos—remainder of refrain and stanza 2
    "Wherever He Leads, I'll Go"
        Tenor Solo—first phrase of stanza 1
        Choir—second phrase of stanza 1
        Tenor Solo—last two phrases of stanza 1
        Choir—Refrain.
           Accompanist modulates to key of A flat
    "Jesus, I My Cross Have Taken"
        Choir—stanza 1 (sung in four parts)
        Choir—stanza 4 (sung in unison)
    "The Way of the Cross Leads Home"
        Choir—Refrain. (Begin with holds over the first two words, "For the"; continue rest of refrain in moderate tempo.)

The Beauty of the Way

READING (by Choral Speaking Choir):
"How beautiful upon the mountains are the feet of him that

bringeth good tidings, that publisheth peace; that bringeth good tidings of good, that publisheth salvation; that saith unto Zion, thy God reigneth!" (Isaiah 52:7).

CHOIR: "How Beautiful Upon the Mountains"—John Stainer

The Conquest of the Way

READING (by Choral Speaking Choir):
"Put on the whole armour of God, that ye may be able to stand against the wiles of the devil. For we wrestle not against flesh and blood, but against principalities, against powers, against the rulers of the darkness of this world, against spiritual wickedness in high places. Wherefore take unto you the whole armour of God, that ye may be able to withstand in the evil day, and having done all, to stand" (Ephesians 6:11-13).

CHOIR: "Onward, Christian Soldiers"—Arr. by Harry Simeone (Fred Waring Arrangement)

The End of the Way

READING (by Choral Speaking Choir):
"I have fought a good fight, I have finished my course, I have kept the faith: henceforth there is laid up for me a crown of righteousness, which the Lord, the righteous judge, shall give me at that day: and not to me only, but unto all them also that love his appearing" (2 Timothy 4:7-8).

CHOIR: "I'll Take My Staff and Travel On"—White Spiritual, arr. by R. Deane Shure

The Triumph of the Way

READING (by Choral Speaking Choir):
"And I heard as it were the voice of a great multitude, and as the voice of many waters, and as the voice of mighty thunderings, saying, Alleluia: for the Lord God omnipotent reigneth" (Revelation 19:6).

CHOIR: "Hallelujah Chorus," from *The Messiah*—George Frederick Handel

Service 39

HERE WE COME A-CAROLING[1]

(A Carol Service for Choir)

PROGRAM

Introduction

"Here We Come A-Caroling"—Old English Wassail Song

(Choir)

Pagan Carol

"The Holly and the Ivy"—Traditional (Story—p. 70)

(Solo)

Legendary Carols

"The Cherry Tree Carol"—Traditional (Story—p. 60)
   (Soloists sing parts of Mary, Joseph, and the Angel)
"O Christmas Tree"—German folk song (Story—See added
   script)
"Good King Wenceslas"—Traditional (Story—p. 64)
(Tenor and Soprano soloists sing parts of King and Page)

(Choir)

The Origin of Carol Singing—Reading   (See added script)

Mystery Play Carols   .

---

1. Unless otherwise indicated, the carols and stories of the carols used in this service
will be found in *The Christmas Carolers' Book in Song and Story*, by Torstein O. Kvamme.
Additional script has been added in some instances to augment the story material. As
much or as little of the story content may be used as the time permits.

Introduction (See added script)

"Lully, Lully, Lu"—Old Italian Carol, or

"The Coventry Carol"—16th century English (Stories—p. 56)

(Women's Trio or three-part Choir)

Carols of the Nations

"Lo, How a Rose E'er Blooming"—15th century German (Story —p. 38)

"The First Noel"—16th century French (Story—p. 10)

"God Rest You Merry, Gentlemen"—17th century English (Story —p. 28)

(Choir)

"Thy Little Ones, Dear Lord, Are We"—18th century Danish (Story—p. 48)

(Children's Choir)

"O Little Town of Bethlehem"—19th century American (Story —p. 12)

(Choir and Congregation)

World Carols

"Silent Night" (antiphonal arrangement)—Gruber, arr. by Wetzel (Story—p. 16)

"O Come, All Ye Faithful"—John Reading, arr. by Vincent Novello (Story—p. 8)

(Choir)

Additional Script (to be used with preceding service):

I. LEGEND OF CHRISTMAS TREE

It is the land of Luther that gave us the Christmas tree. Indeed, some say it was Luther, himself. That, wishing to show his wife and children the beauty of the forest, snow-flecked and frost-jeweled, he brought home a little fir tree and decorated it with white and silver, fastening candles on it to make it shine. To this day the Christmas trees in that country are the loveliest in the world, for no toys are hung on their branches. They are all silver and white, shimmering in the light of one crowning star.

But I like better the much older legend of St. Winfred, the "sole wonder" of whose great and good life was finding the first Christmas tree. During his crusade against the pagan Druids, he cut down a giant oak, their holy tree. As it fell backward, "like a tower groaning," there just behind it, unharmed by the fall of the giant god of primeval forests, stood a very young fir tree, pointing a green spire towards the stars. St. Winfred dropped his axe and spoke thus to the people:

"This little tree, a young child of the forest, shall be your holy tree tonight. It is the wood of peace, for your houses are built of fir. It is the sign of endless life, for its leaves are ever green. See how it points towards Heaven. Let this be called the tree of the Christ-child; gather about it, not in the wild woods but in your homes; there it will shelter no deeds of blood, but loving gifts and rites of kindness."

What joy there must be in Heaven as Winfred looks down to see his "sole wonder" brightening corners throughout the world today![1]

II. Origin of Carol Singing

Carol singing, as we know it, originated more than seven hundred years ago, in the gentle child soul of little Francis of Assisi.

In those days religion was at a very low ebb. Heresy was abroad in the land. The services of the Church were conducted in a language the people did not understand; the Bible was locked up in an unknown tongue; what little preaching was done gave nothing to the uneducated masses.

And Francis, like Jesus, had compassion on the multitude, and longed to teach them. He knew the common people would hear him gladly; for had he not made himself as one of them? Once he had been a rich young man, but he had renounced all to give to the poor. Now he begged his bread, and labored even as they, building churches with his own torn, bleeding fingers and serving lepers.

Yes, the poor loved him because he was their brother. How, then, could he show them Christ, not as the great Judge, not as a terrible King before whose awful majesty the whole earth shook, but as the Child Jesus, the little Brother of all mankind?

Christmas was approaching. Francis thought wistfully of the cloisters of famous monasteries. Were only the holy men in the great religious houses to see Christ this Christmas? He wept at his work—Francis of the joyous heart! How, he groaned in the dark of sleepless nights, could one show an unlettered peasant people the great mysteries?

Suddenly the answer came. By pictures! By *living* pictures, explained in verse written in the common tongue, and sung by the people themselves! The Christmas story, not *read*, but *realized*.

Soon the bright, homely little songs were composed and set to blithe, lilting tunes that seemed to dance for very joy. And now for the Picture! He wanted it to be so beautiful that the people would never forget it. They never did, nor the generations that came after. This Christmas it will be

1. From "Joy to the World," by Beatrice Plumb, *Christian Herald,* January, 1934. Used by permission of *Christian Herald.*

produced in thousands upon thousands of humble European homes, in great cathedrals, probably in your church and mine. It is now a part of Christmas.

It was the Christmas of 1224 that Francis and his faithful disciples set forth to the little Italian village of Grecia and with great pains prepared in the church a representation of the nativity. He strove to make it a *living* picture. Living people represented Mary and Joseph; living animals, the ox and the ass that were tethered close to a rough manger, real straw littered the floor. When it was finished, Francis said, "This they can read."

On Christmas Eve the villagers came to the church—to Bethlehem! And when they saw the old, old story thus portrayed, and heard Francis and his choir singing it, not in scholars' Latin but in words they could understand, old records tell us "They poured forth constant praise to God for His wondrous love to man."

Poor inarticulate peasants! Now the floodgates were open the song burst out in a torrent there was no stemming. It rose and rose. All night long they sang, while Francis stood by the manger, "softly sighing for joy," and giving God thanks that by this simple means the hearts of the people had been touched and taught.

When morning came and they must go home, they sang on the way. And thus the carol, secluded in the cloister for a thousand years, was brought to the shepherds' fields again.[2]

III. INTRODUCTION TO MYSTERY PLAY CAROLS:

Centuries later, carols crossed the Continent to England—but with typical British conservatism, they were kept within sacred walls. They were first sung only between the acts of Christmas mystery pageants given in the parish church. Then, because of their growing hold on the people, they were made a part of the pageant itself. Soon the carolers were vying with the actors for favor. Until one happy evening the singers, swept by a great wave of mounting enthusiasm, left the platform and marched down the centre aisle, singing as they went. Instead of circling the church and returning to the chancel, they marched clear through the door and went parading down the streets with the entire congregation streaming after them, all lustily singing! And from that moment on, carols were in the English streets![3]

2. From "We Have Seen His Star," by Beatrice Plumb, *Christian Herald,* December, 1933. Used by permission of *Christian Herald.*

3. Ibid.

SERVICE 40

"LED BY A STAR"[1]

(A Christmas Service for Choir)

PROGRAM

CHOIR: O Come, O Come, Emmanuel.....................
.......................Gregorian Melody, 8th century
There's a Song in the Air . . Oley Speaks, arr. by Carl Deis
CANTATA: Led by a Star—J. Lilian Vandevere and Haydn M. Morgan

The Shepherds

BARITONE SOLO: In the Field
CHOIR: While Shepherds Watched ....Book of Psalms, 1592
ALTO AND TENOR SOLOS AND CHOIR:
    The Angel and the Shepherd ....Old French Noel
CHOIR: Sing We Noel..............16th century French Carol
BARITONE SOLO, MALE QUARTET AND CHOIR:
    On to Bethlehem ....Haydn M. Morgan

The Wise Men

SOLOS: The Golden Carol................Haydn M. Morgan
The Child Jesus

CHOIR: What Child Is This?..Traditional Tune, "Greensleeves"
SOPRANO SOLO: Mary's Lullaby...........Haydn M. Morgan
SOLO AND CHORUS: Sleep, Holy Babe ....John B. Dykes

---

1. Permission to reprint names and numbers from the Christmas Cantata, *Led by a Star*, by J. Lilian Vandevere and Haydn M. Morgan, granted by C. C. Birchard & Company, publishers.

At the Manger

WOMEN'S CHOIR: Come, Rouse Ye, Lads and Lasses........
.... Bearnais Carol

World Hope

CHOIR: O Come, All Ye Faithful ....John Reading

SCRIPT
(to be used with above program)

CHOIR: O Come, O Come, Emmanuel

1ST READER: Luke 2:1-7

CHOIR: There's a Song in the Air

CANTATA: Led by a Star

The Shepherds

2ND READER: Luke 2:8-14

BARITONE SOLO: In the Field

CHOIR: While Shepherds Watched

ALTO AND TENOR SOLOS AND CHOIR: The Angel and the Shepherd

CHOIR: Sing We Noel

1ST READER:

> All my heart this night rejoices,
> As I hear,
> Far and near,
> Sweetest angel voices:
> "Christ is born" their choirs are singing,
> Till the air,
> Everywhere,
> Now with joy is ringing.
>
> Hark! a voice from yonder manger,
> Soft and sweet,
> Doth entreat,
> "Flee from woe and danger;
> Brethren, come; from all that grieves you
> You are freed;
> All you need
> I will surely give you."

Come, then, let us hasten yonder;
Here let all,
Great and small,
Kneel in awe and wonder,
Love Him who with love is yearning;
Hail the Star
That from far
Bright with hope is burning.

—PAUL GERHARDT, Tr. by Catherine Winkworth

BARITONE SOLO, MALE QUARTET, AND CHOIR: On to Bethlehem

The Wise Men

2ND READER: Matthew 2:1-11

SOLOS: The Golden Carol

1ST READER:

As with gladness men of old
Did the guiding star behold;
As with joy they hailed its light,
Leading onward, beaming bright;
So, most gracious Lord, may we
Evermore be led to Thee.

As with joyful steps they sped
To that lowly manger-bed,
There to bend the knee before
Him whom heaven and earth adore;
So may we with willing feet
Ever seek Thy mercy-seat.

As they offered gifts most rare
At that manger rude and bare,
So may we with holy joy,
Pure and free from sin's alloy,
All our costliest treasures bring,
Christ, to Thee, our heavenly King.

—WILLIAM C. DIX

(Interlude of quiet organ or piano music. If desired, a love offering may be taken here.)

The Child Jesus

2ND READER:

Down from a sky of silver stars
Floated a star of gold;
Trembling, it floated low and stood
Over an humble fold.
It was the quiet time before
The angel choir began,
Before the Wise Men bowed them down
To the little Son of Man.
The Star came closer down the hill,
It bloomed in the courtyard tree.
And, leaning to find, as mothers will,
What manner of child was He,
Mary murmured, "It is so dark,
His face I cannot see . . ."
The door swung in on a wind of light.
No darkness was left at all,
And Mary saw that her child was God,
By a star on a stable wall![2]

—MAY WILLIAMS WARD

CHOIR: What Child Is This?

SOPRANO SOLO: Mary's Lullaby

CHOIR: Sleep, Holy Babe

At the Manger
(Optional Selection for a Verse Speaking Choir)

YOUNG SHEPHERDS (lighter voices):

The hay is deep and softly warm
    Against the winter cold,
He rests like any little lamb,
    Within the shepherd's fold.
How still, how very still he lies,
    With tiny fingers curled.
A lowly manger proudly holds
    The Saviour of the world.

OLDER SHEPHERDS (deeper voices):

How strange that song the angel sang,
    Of "Peace on earth—Good-Will!"
'Tis quiet here, but through the air,
And in our hearts, and everywhere,
    That song is ringing still.

---

2. "The Star Stood Over," by May Williams Ward. Used by permission of the author and the *Kansas City Star*.

WISE MEN (deep voices):

> We looked for signs of kingly power,
>   For purple robes, and gold,
> And lo, we find an infant here,
>   Whom swaddling clothes enfold.
> Enrapt we gaze full silently
>   Upon the splendid sight.
> In reverent wonder, here we stand,
> The while he lifts his tiny hand
>   In majesty and might.

YOUNG SHEPHERDS

> But why should we be standing here,
>   And stay on bended knee?
> Run quickly! Tell it far and near
>   That all should come and see.
> The village should not slumber—
>   Arise, and call the folk!
> Repeat to them the joyful song
>   We heard when we awoke.
> Go up and down the quiet street,
>   Tell out the news, and then repeat.
> Come! Come this happy morn!
>   Come, children, unto Bethlehem,
> For Christ, the Lord, is born![3]

—J. LILIAN VANDEVERE

TREBLE CHOIR: Come, Rouse Ye, Lads and Lasses

World Hope

1ST READER:

"Did you think The Star was meant just for the Magi and the Shepherds, just for that one night alone? Ah, no! God hung it there against the ages; it is for all of us. Its radiance enfolds us all, knowing no bound or creed, color or servitude. It guides the aged home; it is reflected in the eyes of babes, generation after generation, and in the eyes of mothers seeking in their babes the countenance of Christ. All, all of us are come once more under

---

3. From the Cantata, *Led by a Star*, C. C. Birchard & Company, Boston, Massachusetts. Reprinted by permission.

the spell of The Star, come to take new hope in peace and the Prince of Peace!"[4]

2ND READER:

> For unto us a child is born,
> Unto us a son is given:
> And the government shall be upon his shoulder:
> And his name shall be called Wonderful, Counsellor,
> The mighty God, The everlasting Father,
> The Prince of Peace.
>
> —ISAIAH 9:6

CHOIR: O Come, All Ye Faithful

For other services adaptable for choir use, see the following services:

In Part One (Section I):
   "God Give Me Mountains"
   "The Lord Is My Shepherd"
In Part One (Section II):
   "Windows of the Soul"
In Part Two:
   "Let There Be Light"
   "We Have Seen His Star"

---

4. "We Have Seen His Star," from *Christian Herald,* December, 1947. Used by permission of *Christian Herald.*

I AM YOUR HYMNAL

I am your Hymnal.

I spend my days in the rack in front of you or on the seat beside you and I am always at your command.

When you reach for me I am always there, ready to open at your will.

By the mystery of the printer's art I have shared the wisdom and the ideals of the ages and hold them in store ready to let them leap, at your will, from my pages to nestle in your responsive heart.

The beautiful vision of the poets, the heartthrobs of the mystics, the dreams of the prophets, and the constructive purpose of the social pioneer—all these are mine—to be made yours.

Men of your own faith, and those of other great faiths, broaden your life as they speak to you through me.

By the strange art of printed signs and symbols great music has been captured as it overflowed the souls of the musicians of all times and is released from me to tremble in the air about you and enter your life.

I am your Hymnal.

—PERCY R. HAYWARD

Used by permission of the author.

PART IV

VARIED USES

OF

HYMNS

I

"LINING OUT" A HYMN

The following gospel song is here used in the manner known as "lining out" a hymn. Several methods of presentation are possible, such as the following:

1. The leader reads the related Scripture passage, and the group sings a line of the hymn.

2. The Scripture passages are numbered and passed out to different members of the group to be read at the indicated times.

3. The whole service is printed and placed in the hands of the group, who participate in the entire service, singing the hymn and reading the Scripture passages in unison.

4. The entire service may be presented by a soloist and a reader, with or without group participation on the singing of the refrain.

The refrain is to be sung in its entirety at the conclusion of each stanza.

"God Will Take Care Of You"[1]

Stanza 1

SCRIPTURE: "The eternal God is thy refuge, and underneath are the everlasting arms" (Deuteronomy 33:27).

LINE 1: "Be not dismayed whate'er betide, God will take care of you."

SCRIPTURE: "He shall cover thee with his feathers, and under his wings shalt thou trust: his truth shall be thy shield and buckler" (Psalm 91:4).

LINE 2: "Beneath his wings of love abide, God will take care of you."

---

1. Words of hymn quoted by permission of Hope Publishing Co.

REFRAIN: "God will take care of you,
Through every day, o'er all the way,
He will take care of you,
God will take care of you."

Stanza 2

SCRIPTURE: "Now when he had left speaking, he said unto Simon, Launch out into the deep, and let down your nets for a draught. And Simon answering said unto him, Master, we have toiled all the night, and have taken nothing: nevertheless at thy word I will let down the net. And when they had this done, they inclosed a great multitude of fishes: and their net brake" (Luke 5:4-6).

LINE 1: "Thro' days of toil when heart doth fail, God will take care of you."

SCRIPTURE: "Thou shalt not be afraid for the terror by night; nor for the arrow that flieth by day; nor for the pestilence that walketh in darkness; nor for the destruction that wasteth at noonday. For he shall give his angels charge over thee, to keep thee in all thy ways. They shall bear thee up in their hands, lest thou dash thy foot against a stone" (Psalm 91:5-6, 11-12).

LINE 2: "When dangers fierce your path assail, God will take care of you."

REFRAIN

Stanza 3

SCRIPTURE: "My God shall supply all your need according to his riches in glory by Christ Jesus" (Philippians 4:19).

LINE 1: "All you may need he will provide, God will take care of you."

SCRIPTURE: "And all things, whatsoever ye shall ask in prayer, believing, ye shall receive" (Matthew 21:22).

LINE 2: "Nothing you ask will be denied, God will take care of you."

REFRAIN

Stanza 4

SCRIPTURE: "There hath no temptation taken you but such as is common to man: but God is faithful, who will not suffer you to be tempted above that ye are able; but will with the temptation also make a way to escape, that ye may be able to bear it" (1 Corinthians 10:13).

LINE 1: "No matter what may be the test, God will take care of you."

SCRIPTURE: "Come unto me, all ye that labour and are heavy laden, and I will give you rest. Take my yoke upon you, and learn of me; for I am meek and lowly in heart: and ye shall find rest unto your souls. For my yoke is easy, and my burden is light" (Matthew 11:28-30).

LINE 2: "Lean, weary one, upon his breast, God will take care of you."

REFRAIN

II

HYMN—SCRIPTURE COMBINATION

Another variation in the use of hymns may be found in alternating Scripture passages with the different stanzas of a hymn which express the same thought.

The following combination of the Psalm of Moses (Psalm 90) with Isaac Watts's hymn, "O God, Our Help in Ages Past," which is a paraphrase of this psalm, illustrates this method of alternating hymn stanzas with Scripture.

"Lord, thou hast been our dwelling place in all generations" (Psalm 90:1).

> O God, our help in ages past,
> Our hope for years to come,
> Our shelter from the stormy blast,
> And our eternal home.

"Before the mountains were brought forth, or ever thou hadst formed the earth and the world, even from everlasting to everlasting, thou art God" (Psalm 90:2).

> Before the hills in order stood,
> Or earth received her frame,
> From everlasting Thou art God,
> To endless years the same.

"For a thousand years in thy sight are but as yesterday when it is past, and as a watch in the night" (Psalm 90:4).

> A thousand ages in Thy sight
> Are like an evening gone;
> Short as the watch that ends the night
> Before the rising sun.

"The days of our years are threescore and ten; and if by reason of strength they be fourscore years, yet is their strength labour and sorrow; for it is soon cut off, and we fly away. So teach us to number our days, that we may apply our hearts unto wisdom" (Psalm 90:10-12).

> Time, like an ever-rolling stream,
> Bears all its sons away;
> They fly, forgotten, as a dream
> Dies at the opening day.

"O satisfy us early with thy mercy; that we may rejoice and be glad all our days. Make us glad according to the days wherein thou hast afflicted us, and the years wherein we have seen evil. And let the beauty of the Lord our God be upon us: and establish thou the work of our hands upon us; yea, the work of our hands establish thou it" (Psalm 90:14-15, 17).

> O God, our help in ages past,
> Our hope for years to come,
> Be Thou our guard while life shall last,
> And our eternal home.

(H. Augustine Smith's book, *Lyric Religion,* contains a number of excellent hymn and Scripture responsive services.)

III

BIBLE STORIES WITH HYMNS

The following illustrates a plan in which a familiar Bible story is given a new and more vivid interpretation through the use of appropriate hymn selections to be sung by the entire group to further illustrate certain points in the story. Too often these Bible stories lose their significance and fail to hold the interest of those who have often heard them read; this new approach to them, especially preceding a comprehensive study of the passage, would do much to arouse a new interest in them.

SCRIPTURE PASSAGE: Acts 16:9-34

Verse 9—"Send the Light" (stanza 1)

Verse 10—"Send the Light" (stanza 2)

Verses 11-13—"Sweet Hour of Prayer" (stanza 1)

Verses 14-15—"Blest Be the Tie" (stanzas 1, 2)

Verses 16-18—"Take the Name of Jesus with You" (stanza 1)

Verses 19-24—"Jesus, I My Cross Have Taken" (stanzas 1, 3)

Verse 25—"O for a Thousand Tongues to Sing" (stanzas 1, 3, 4)

Verses 26-31—"Only Trust Him" (stanza 3)

Verse 32—"Wonderful Words of Life" (stanza 2)

Verses 33-34—"O Happy Day" (stanza 1), or "Blessed Assurance" (stanza 1)

IV

BIBLE CHARACTERIZATIONS WITH HYMNS

Occasionally, a worship service may contain characterizations of certain Bible characters; one preceding the Sunday school lesson study of a Bible character or characters would arouse interest in the study which is to follow.

The following Scripture passages and hymns are suggested to fit certain events in the lives of some of the followers of Jesus. The worshipers are to think of the hymns as being the vocal expression of the Bible character himself as he reacts to the situation related in the preceding Scripture passage.

First disciples of Jesus:
    Scripture: Matthew 4:18-22
    Hymn: "Footsteps of Jesus" (stanzas 1, 2, 3)

Mary, sister of Lazarus and Martha:
    Scripture: Luke 10:38-42
    Hymn: "More Love to Thee, O Christ" (stanza 1)

The Syrophenician Woman:
    Scripture: Mark 7:24-30
    Hymn: "Pass Me Not, O Gentle Saviour" (stanza 1)

James and John, disciples of Jesus:
    Scripture: Matthew 20:20-22
    Hymn: "Are Ye Able?" (stanza 1)

Simon Peter:
    Scripture: Luke 22:31-34
    Hymn: "In the Hour of Trial" (stanza 1)

Mary Magdalene:
    Scripture: John 20:11-16
    Hymn: "In the Garden" (all stanzas)

V

HYMN—PRAYER COMBINATION

Since many of our greatest hymns are in themselves fervent prayers, hymns can often be used as prayers. Such hymns may be used as preludes at the opening of a service to create an atmosphere of prayer; they may be played after a spoken prayer to continue the season of prayer; or they may be sung or read as a sub-

stitute for the usual spoken prayer. Examples of typical prayer
hymns are found in "Dear Lord and Father of Mankind," "Speak
to My Heart, Lord Jesus," "Breathe On Me," "Lead, Kindly Light,"
"More Love to Thee," "Jesus, Saviour, Pilot Me," "I Need Thee
Every Hour," and "Have Thine Own Way, Lord." In these, as well
as in many others, the tunes and words combine to produce the
desired emotional response.

Young people might carry out a project of studying the tunes
of the hymns in the hymnal to select those with outstanding prayer
value. They might be classified under headings such as joyful
praise, deep penitence, quiet waiting upon God. The words of the
hymns may also be thus studied and classified, selecting those which
may be used instead of extemporaneous prayers.

A hymn and prayer combination such as the following might be
used at times as one phase of a worship program. The hymn here
used is an evening worship hymn, and is combined with a few Bible
prayers to be used as a musical benediction for an evening service.

"Saviour, Again to Thy Dear Name We Raise"

> Saviour, again to Thy dear name we raise
> With one accord our parting hymn of praise;
> We stand to bless Thee ere our worship cease,
> Then, lowly kneeling, wait Thy word of peace.

"I will hear what God the Lord will speak: for he will speak
peace unto his people, and to his saints" (Psalm 85:8).

"Peace I leave with you, my peace I give unto you: not as the
world giveth, give I unto you. Let not your heart be troubled,
neither let it be afraid" (John 14:27).

> Grant us Thy peace, Lord, through the coming night,
> With Thee began, with Thee shall end the day;
> Guard Thou the lips from sin, the hearts from shame,
> That in this house have called upon Thy name.

"Let my prayer be set forth before thee as incense; and the lift-
ing up of my hands as the evening sacrifice. Set a watch, O Lord,
before my mouth; keep the door of my lips. Incline not my heart
to any evil thing, to practice wicked works with men that work iniquity. . . . Mine eyes are unto thee, O God the Lord: in thee is
my trust; leave not my soul destitute" (Psalm 141:2-4, 8).

Grant us Thy peace, Lord, through the coming night,
Turn Thou for us its darkness into light;
From harm and danger keep Thy children free,
For dark and light are both alike to Thee.

"I will both lay me down in peace, and sleep: for thou, Lord, only makest me dwell in safety" (Psalm 4:8).

Grant us Thy peace throughout our earthly life,
Our balm in sorrow, and our stay in strife;
Then, when Thy voice shall bid our conflict cease,
Call us, O Lord, to Thine eternal peace.

"Now the God of peace, that brought again from the dead our Lord Jesus, that great shepherd of the sheep, through the blood of the everlasting covenant, make you perfect in every good work to do his will, working in you that which is well-pleasing in his sight, through Jesus Christ; to whom be glory for ever and ever. Amen" (Hebrews 13:20-21).

VI

HYMN—QUOTATION COMBINATION

Occasionally it may be fitting to combine brief quotations with hymns to carry out a certain theme. The following brief devotional service is an example of such a plan, and may be used as a challenge to service. The quotations will impress themselves upon the minds of the participants in the service more readily if they are printed, together with names and stanzas of the hymns, and placed in the hands of those taking part. The group itself may be asked to read the quotations in unison, or they may be read by the leader or by several individuals if preferred.

HYMN: "Hark, the Voice of Jesus Calling" (stanza 1)

GROUP: "God becomes a reality to us when He lays upon us a commission" (Author Unknown).

HYMN: "Jesus Calls Us" (stanzas 1, 4)

GROUP: "It is not the possession of extraordinary gifts that makes extraordinary usefulness, but the dedication of what we have to the service of God" (F. W. Robertson).

HYMN: "Where He Leads Me" (stanza 1), or
      "Give of Your Best to the Master" (stanza 2)

GROUP: "All service ranks the same with God . . .
       There is no last nor first" (Browning).

HYMN: "Our Best" (stanza 1)

GROUP: "To turn all we possess into the channels of universal love
       becomes the business of our lives" (John Woolman).

HYMN: "O Master, Let Me Walk with Thee" (stanzas 1, 2), or
      "Make Me a Channel of Blessing" (stanza 1)

GROUP: "The serene, silent beauty of a holy life is the most power-
       ful influence in the world, next to the might of God"
       (Pascal).

HYMN: "Let Others See Jesus in You" (stanzas 1, 2)

GROUP: "He who forgets self in the service of others will be abun-
       dantly rewarded" (Author Unknown).

HYMN: "It Pays to Serve Jesus" (stanzas 1, 2)

GROUP: "The great use of life is to spend it for something that will
       outlast it" (William James).

HYMN: "To the Work" (stanzas 1, 2)

VII

HYMNS AS UNISON AND RESPONSIVE READINGS

Hymns may be used very effectively as unison or responsive readings, i.e., reading the words of the hymn in unison or responsively,
sometimes only one or two stanzas, sometimes the entire poem. Some
hymns are difficult to sing for congregational use, but the beauty
of the words makes the reading of them a valuable addition to any
service. With small groups, this may be done to the accompaniment
of quiet music, such as "Lead, Kindly Light" to the music of "Lux
Benigna," "Take My Life and Let It Be" to "Elleston," "O Love
That Wilt Not Let Me Go" to "St. Margaret."

VIII

HYMNS AS ECHO MUSIC

Occasionally echo music may be used to enrich the worship service. This may be performed by a soloist or a group of singers, stationed outside the room in which the service is being held. This echo music is even more effective if heard coming from outside the church, perhaps from a window or an outside door.

Echo music may be used in various ways. The group of worshipers may sing two stanzas of a certain hymn, after which the echo singers sing very softly the last stanza. If the song selected has a long refrain, they may repeat this chorus only. At times it is effective to have the echo gradually diminish in volume toward the end, giving the effect of the singers marching away into the distance. Occasionally a musical instrument, such as a violin, trumpet, or cornet, may be used to produce the echo effect when played in a room far enough away to give the impression of distance.

A few hymns adaptable for echo effects are here suggested:

(1) "Still, Still with Thee" (Echo on last stanza)

(2) "Day Is Dying in the West" (Echo of refrain repeated after congregation sings stanza and refrain.)

(3) "Sun of My Soul" (Congregation sings first and third stanzas; echo on second and fourth stanzas.)

(4) "Silent Night, Holy Night" (Congregation and echo singers sing alternate phrases,—"Silent night,—holy night,—all is calm,—all is bright," throughout the first stanza; congregation sings second and third stanzas; echo singers sing last stanza in its entirety, or alternately with the congregation as the first.)

(5) "There Is a Green Hill Far Away" (Refrain sung by echo singers after congregation sings each stanza.)

IX

HYMNS USED ANTIPHONALLY

Some lovely effects may be secured by antiphonal singing of hymns, although such a practice should not be overdone. This is a question and answer method, one group singing a phrase, section, or stanza of the hymn, after which another group answers with the next section and so on. Merely to seek to "pep up" a group or to produce competition between two groups, such as boys against girls, etc., defeats the purpose of such a plan. It should be remembered that its principal purpose is to lend beauty and variety to the worship service; to produce, not to destroy, the worshipful atmosphere; and to enhance the message of the words in the minds of the worshipers. If these ideals are kept in mind, the antiphonal effect should contribute definitely to the worship experience.

Certain hymns lend themselves to such usage more than others. The following are suggested as adaptable to such a plan: .

(1) "I Heard the Voice of Jesus Say"

     1st Group:—Represent the Christian as he hears the voice of Jesus and responds.

     2nd Group:—Represent the voice of Jesus and sing portions of hymn which contain his words.

(2) "O Jesus, Thou Art Standing"

     1st Group:—Sing first half of each stanza.

     2nd Group:—Sing second half of each stanza.

(3) "Watchman, Tell Us of the Night"

     1st Group:—Sing the question, "Watchman, tell us of the night, what its signs of promise are?"

     2nd Group:—Sing the answer, "Trav'ler, o'er yon mountain height, see that glory-beaming star."

     Continue in this manner throughout the song.

     (See *Lyric Religion* by H. Augustine Smith for special services utilizing this hymn.)

(4) "Are Ye Able?"

     1st Group:—Sing questions contained in the stanzas.

     2nd Group:—Sing answer contained in the refrain.

(5) "For the Beauty of the Earth"

     Women's Voices:—"For the beauty of the earth"

     Men's Voices:—"For the glory of the skies"

     Women's Voices:—"For the love which from our birth"

Men's Voices:—"Over and around us lies"
All Voices:—"Lord of all, to Thee we raise this our hymn
    of grateful praise."
Continue above plan throughout all stanzas.

X

HYMNS WITH STORIES

Another very valuable method of using hymns is the use of stories
with them. Paul wrote to the Corinthians, "I will sing with the
spirit, and I will sing with the understanding also" (1 Corinthians
14:15). To know by whom and under what circumstances a hymn
was written, who composed the music that carries the words on
wings of song, and what the hymn has meant to needy hearts who
have heard and sung its message, will do much to increase our
ability to sing with the spirit and the understanding as Paul ex-
horts the worshiper to do.

It is worth while to bring people into touch with the lives of such
hymn writers as John Newton, Isaac Watts, Charles Wesley, and
Fanny Crosby. An interesting variation in a worship program would
be to present a song service called, "An Hour With Hymn Writers,"
or a "Charles Wesley," or a "Fanny Crosby" program.

There is also an unlimited field in the stories of what hymns have
done, and this is a field of great interest and rare adventure to
young people. Uncounted hundreds of men and women, boys and
girls, have been touched by the message of a hymn when the spoken
word has failed, and stories telling of this fruitful ministry are
abundant. These simple little stories are of great value, giving those
who hear them new interest in the hymns they sing, and teaching
them the power of hymns over the lives of men and women everywhere.

The tunes of hymns have stories as well as the words, and "An
Evening with the Tunes" would also add variety to a worship program in which Christians engage. Another suggested use is to have
a "hymn-for-the-month," and with that hymn to present the history

of the hymn, the biography of the author and the composer, and any interesting experiences concerning the writing or use of the hymn.

There are numbers of good books which contain valuable material wherein the above information concerning the authors and stories of hymns may be found. The following are suggested for those who wish to pursue this subject further:

Fanny Crosby's Story of Ninety-four Years, S. Trevena Jackson (Rodeheaver Hall-Mack Co.)

Forty Gospel Hymn Stories, George W. Sanville (Rodeheaver Hall-Mack Co.)

Hymn Interpretations, Charles C. Washburn (Abingdon-Cokesbury)

Hymns in the Lives of Men, Robert Guy McCutchan (Abingdon-Cokesbury)

Hymn Stories of the 20th Century, William J. Hart (W. A. Wilde Co.)

Hymns That Endure, W. Thorburn Clark (Broadman)

Know Your Hymns?, Quiz Book on Hymns—Frederick Hall (W. A. Wilde Co.)

Lyric Religion, H. Augustine Smith (Fleming Revell)

More Hymn Stories, Carl F. Price (Abingdon-Cokesbury)

One Hundred and One Hymn Stories, Carl F. Price (Abingdon-Cokesbury)

Our Hymnody, Robert Guy McCutchan (Abingdon-Cokesbury)

Stories of Fadeless Hymns, W. Thorburn Clark (Broadman)

Stories of Favorite Hymns, Kathleen Blanchard (Zondervan)

Stories of Great Hymn Writers, Ivan H. Hagedorn (Zondervan)

Stories of Popular Hymns, Kathleen Blanchard (Zondervan)

Stories of Hymns We Love, Cecilia Margaret Rudin (John Rudin & Co.)

Hymn Programs, Companion Book to *Stories of Hymns We Love*

Two Hundred Hymn Stories, Ellen Jane Lorenz (Lorenz)

Unfamiliar Stories of Familiar Hymns, William J. Hart (W. A. Wilde Co.)

XI

HYMNS WITH PICTURES

Famous pictures combined with famous hymns and used together, with or without the stories of each, make hymns live in a new and vivid way. Cynthia Pearl Maus, in *Christ and the Fine Arts* says: "The use of great pictures in teaching religious concepts rests upon the sound educational principle that a truth which reaches the mind through the eye-gate and the ear-gate at the same time doubles the impression." She believes that "if young people and adults will pay the price to make great masterpieces of religious art live, through an artistic presentation of the artist's message in story, accompanied with music and a reproduction of the picture, they may become co-workers with Christ in making truth and beauty so attractive that the unseeing will be led to follow Him, whom to know aright is life abundant here and life eternal hereafter."[1]

Several combinations of hymns and art masterpieces which may be used together are here suggested: "Work, for the Night Is Coming" with Millet's *The Sower;* "Now the Day Is Over" with Millet's *The Angelus;* "Silent Night" with Correggio's *Holy Night;* "Christ the Lord Is Risen Today" with Ender's *Holy Women at the Tomb;* "Jesus Calls Us" with Zimmermann's *Christ and the Fishermen;* "O Jesus, Thou Art Standing" with Holman Hunt's *The Light of the World;* "Fairest Lord Jesus" with Sallman's *Head of Christ;* "What a Friend We Have in Jesus" with Hofmann's *At the Home of Mary and Martha.*

The following books contain much valuable material concerning the use of art and music in religion:

Worship Programs in the Fine Arts for Young People, Alice A. Bays (Abingdon-Cokesbury)

Famous Hymns: With Stories and Pictures, Elizabeth Hubbard Bonsall (American Sunday School Union) Best for children.

Christ and the Fine Arts, Cynthia Pearl Maus (Harper and Brothers)

The World's Great Madonnas, Cynthia Pearl Maus, (Harper and Brothers)

---

1. From *Christ and the Fine Arts,* Maus, pp. 5-9. Copyright, 1938. Published by Harper & Brothers, New York 16, N. Y. Used by special permission of the author.

The ninety masterpieces of art included in *Christ and the Fine Arts* may be secured in S. V. E. filmstrip series in black and white, while fifty-seven of them are now available in color slides.

One hundred and fourteen pictures from *The World's Great Madonnas* are available in a series of seven filmstrips in black and white. These filmstrips contain world-famous masterpieces of the Madonnas of the world.

All of the above films are obtainable from the Society of Visual Education, Inc., 100 East Ohio Street, Chicago 11, Illinois, or from most denominational supply houses.

Since these two books correlate famous hymns and carols with interpretations of the great masterpieces of art, the use of the above films with the suggested music should afford unlimited possibilities for attractive worship programs. Worship leaders will be well re-paid for the cost and labor connected with the building of such worship services.

Filmstrips and color slides of many hymns may also be secured from the Society of Visual Education, Inc. They publish a pamphlet entitled *Library of Religious Kodachromes and 2"x2" Color Slides*, with full information concerning films of the leading producers of religious visual materials; or such information can be secured from most religious publishing houses. Church musicians will be interested in their filmstrips and color slides of many of the great hymns of the church, the use of which can do much to promote better group singing in the church. Some of these contain the words of the hymns, either on a plain or an illustrated background, in black and white or in color; others contain the words and music exactly as they appear in the hymnbook.

The Baptist Book Store issues a catalogue of audio-visual aids entitled *Focus*, which contains information concerning the purchase of all kinds of visual materials. In it will be found information concerning (1) slide sets of biblical and missionary pictures, pictures dealing with subjects such as Prayer, Bible, Brotherhood, Kingdom of Heaven, etc.; (2) hymn strips of almost any hymn desired; and (3) reproductions of many of the great art masterpieces, framed or unframed, in all sizes.

Another use which may be made of this combination of materials is the use of chalk talks with hymns. A valuable book containing information concerning this type of visual aid will be found in *Illustrated Hymn Talks,* by Stella O. Barnett, with devotionals by Susan Adams, published by Fleming H. Revell Co. This contains illustrations and devotionals utilizing sixteen well-known hymns with chalk talks.

XII

HYMNS DRAMATIZED AND PANTOMIMED

Another method which will lend variety and new meaning to hymns is the dramatization or pantomiming of them.

Walter H. Baker Company publishes some interesting dramatizations of hymns and hymn writers as follows:

1. *Living Hymns*—Edith H. Willis and Edith Ellsworth

   A Choral Drama depicting the centuries of struggle which lie behind our best-loved hymns and hymn writers, to be presented by two narrators, one or more choruses or choirs, and accompanist. This may be given as a full-hour program, or as a series of four twenty-minute presentations. Full directions are given for use with large or small groups. No scenery or costume requirements.

2. *The Birth of the Song, "Silent Night"*—Florence Felton French

   A dramatization of the story back of the writing of the world's most beloved Christmas carol. Required for production: Narrator, six characters, organ and guitar music and choir.

   This play will also be found in *Treasury of Religious Plays,* edited by Thelma Sharman Brown (Association Press).

3. *The Songs of Christmas*—A Play with Carols and Tableaux—Martha Bayly Shannon

   This play can be produced by young people with minimum number of rehearsals, a very simple setting and few properties. Time required for full program, one hour. Required for production: Eight characters, five groups consisting of English Waits, Bethlehem Children, Bethlehem Women, Angels and Modern Carolers. All musical numbers will be found in *The*

Christmas Carolers' Book in Song and Story by Torstein O. Kvamme.

Lorenz Publishing Company publishes a biographical play on the life of the blind hymn writer, Fanny Crosby. It is entitled, *Fanny Crosby,* by Marcus Bach; right of performance is granted only to those who purchase eight or more copies. Requires narrator and seven characters, quartet, and organ music.

Dramatized stories of many hymns and hymn writers will be found in two valuable books entitled *Dramatized Stories of Hymns and Hymn Writers,* and *More Dramatized Stories of Hymns and Hymn Writers* by Ernest K. Emurian, published by W. A. Wilde Company.

Each of these contains sixteen nonroyalty plays which dramatize the true stories back of many of our well-known hymns as well as giving interesting information from the lives of the hymn writers.

Selections from *Dramatized Stories of Hymns and Hymn Writers* are also published in paper-bound form, two plays to each book.

In *Lyric Religion,* by H. Augustine Smith, dramatizations for four hymns will be found. They are, "Fling Out the Banner," "In the Cross of Christ I Glory," "The Day of Resurrection" (Candlelight Ceremonial), and "Watchman, Tell Us of the Night."

The Eldridge Entertainment House publishes several pantomimes of hymns, which include the following:

1. *Ten Pantomimed Hymns*—Poses by Ida Belle Lull

    Among the hymns included are: "Almost Persuaded," "Let the Lower Lights Be Burning," "Love Lifted Me," "Near the Cross," "The Beautiful Garden of Prayer," "Blest Be the Tie," and "Sometime We'll Understand."

    Some of these are to be presented by children, some by young women, with musical background. Full instructions given.

2. *The Old Rugged Cross*—Mrs. Ray Bentz

    A Pantomime of the well-known hymn, to be presented by a group of young women.

XIII

HYMN—ANTHEM ARRANGEMENTS

There are a number of very fine hymn-anthem arrangements

which can be secured for quartet or choir use. Some of these arrangements provide for certain stanzas of familiar hymns to be sung by the congregation from their hymnals, while other stanzas are given varied treatment, with new music written to the familiar words, to be sung by soloists, quartets, male choir, treble choir, or mixed choir. They may be used also in their entirety by a choir or smaller vocal ensemble, to introduce new hymns to the congregation.

W. B. Olds has made some splendid arrangements of this type which are published by Hall & McCreary Company. Each hymn-anthem is published in separate octavo form; the following hymns may be secured in these arrangements: "Abide with Me," "Alas! and Did My Saviour Bleed?" "A Mighty Fortress Is Our God," "Day Is Dying in the West," "Dear Lord and Father of Mankind," "Faith of Our Fathers," "From Every Stormy Wind That Blows," "Immortal Love, Forever Full," "Jesus Calls Us," "Jesus, I My Cross Have Taken," "Jesus, Saviour, Pilot Me," "Jesus, the Very Thought of Thee," "My Faith Looks Up to Thee," "O Jesus, Thou Art Standing," "O Zion, Haste," "Rock of Ages," "Sun of My Soul," "The King of Love My Shepherd Is," "When I Survey the Wondrous Cross," and "When Morning Gilds the Skies."

The Rodeheaver Hall-Mack Company has published anthem arrangements of a number of familiar gospel songs for mixed choir. Among them are arrangements of "The Old Rugged Cross," "In the Garden," "No One Ever Cared for Me Like Jesus," "My Father Watches Over Me" (combined with "His Eye Is on the Sparrow"), and "Living for Jesus" (combined with "Jesus, Rose of Sharon"). Two such arrangements for male choir or quartet are found in Rodeheaver's publications of "I'd Rather Have Jesus," and "Beyond the Sunset" (combined with "Sunrise Tomorrow").

Another Rodeheaver publication which is worthy of note is a book entitled *Anthem—ets*, for the Youth Choir, Vol. I, compiled and arranged by John Josey. The book contains nine arrangements of hymns with Scripture readings.

Two books with valuable material of this kind may be secured from the Lorenz Publishing Company. They are:

(1) *Hymn—Tune Anthems* (nineteen anthems)

Anthem—Fantasias on *Familiar Hymn Tunes,* compiled by Ellen Jane Lorenz.

(2) *Gospel Song Anthems* (thirty-one anthems—five responses)
Easy anthems for mixed voices based on *Familiar Gospel Songs,* compiled by Ellen Jane Lorenz.

XIV

HYMNS WITH DESCANTS

Another way to awaken new interest in the fine old hymns and to add new beauty and brilliancy to them is to use them occasionally with descants. A descant is a counter melody, to be sung by a choir, a few voices, or a solo voice while the congregation sings the original melody. There are several fine publications of hymns with descants, a few of which are given below.

1. *Great Songs of Faith.* (Neil A. Kjos Music Co.)
   Great hymns arranged with melody and descant, with an occasional third part added.

2. *Great Hymns With Descants,* Edward G. Mead. (Hall & Mc-Creary Co.)
   Twenty-five hymns with descants.

3. *Descants on Familiar Hymns,* Peter C. Lutkin. (H. T. Fitzsimmons Co.)
   Contains eight familiar and widely-used hymns.

4. *Descants on Eight Hymns,* Jeanne Boyd. (H. T. Fitzsimmons Co.)

5. *Descants on Christmas Carols* (for treble and mixed voices) arr. and edited by Mary S. Vernon, Robert Sheehan, and William Hughes.
   H. & M. Auditorium Series No. 47. (Hall & McCreary Co.)

6. *Descants on Ten Christmas Hymns and Carols,* Frances Frothingham. (Clayton F. Summy Co.)

XV

HYMN QUIZ

The following "Dr. H. B. Quiz" could not rightly be called material for a worship service, but it could be used with a group of young people upon certain occasions to arouse a deeper interest in and understanding of the place and purpose of hymns in worship. To make the "speaker" more realistic, the leader may place a music stand with open hymnbook at his side, and "introduce" the "speaker" to the group in a typical introduction, stressing the fact that a "distinguished guest" is to be the "speaker" of the day. The leader may then proceed to give the message of "Dr. H. B." to the group as though another person was the speaker, or he may have another person personify "Dr. H. B." It may be given with or without the quiz; if given with quiz, provide each member of the group with quiz sheets before the service begins.

DR. H. B. SPEAKS

I am Dr. H. B., better known to you as Dr. Hymnbook. Each sabbath day you will find me beside the Bible on every pulpit desk. You will also find me in the pews of every church house, sometimes in holders provided for my use, sometimes on the seats, and sometimes even on the floor! In some churches, and by some people, I am treated with reverence and respect; in other churches I am carelessly thrown about and written in and given less care and thought than the Sunday newspaper! Perhaps this is because so many church people do not realize just what my real value and purpose are in a service of worship. In fact, I sometimes wonder, when I look into their minds as they sing some of my great worship hymns, if some Christians really know what it means to worship.

For instance, just last Sunday, a very beautiful young lady in the congregation was singing "Holy, Holy, Holy, Lord God Almighty, early in the morning my song shall rise to Thee." Her voice was a lovely, rich soprano, but when I peeped into her mind, what do you suppose she was thinking? Not of the holiness of God, but of the new fall hats displayed in the audience that morning, and just what color should she select for her own new bonnet? Surely she did not realize that the hymn which she was singing is a call to worship to thousands of worshipers each Lord's Day the world over, and that in its stately rhythm is to be heard the drumbeat of the church of God as it voices its faith in "God in Three Persons, Blessed Trinity."

In fact, I have come to believe, from the use which Christian worshipers make of me every Sunday, that the great majority of them think or know little or nothing about what they are singing. I find some of them singing, "Beneath the cross of Jesus I fain would take my stand," when they have taken their stand with the worldly, pleasure-seeking crowd the Saturday night before; I hear others expressing a desire for "A thousand tongues to sing my great Redeemer's praise" when they do not even use the one tongue God has given them to speak his praise or tell of his grace the whole week through. I hear some Christians promising God, "I'll go where you want me to go, dear Lord" who have no intention whatsoever of keeping that promise; others I hear praying for "More love to Thee, O Christ," when in their hearts there is no attitude nor thought of prayer, nor desire for more love to Christ or anyone else. Surely God must rejoice when he finds a worshiper in his house of worship who does sincerely worship him and pray to him as he sings a song of praise or of prayer from my pages.

If I could "speak with the tongues of men and of angels," I would like to tell every Christian the world over that the only purpose of my being in existence is that I might serve as a medium of expression through which the Christian may express his worship, his praise, his aspiration, and his prayer to God. If those who sing from my pages merely sing the notes mechanically, with little or no thought given to the words that constitute my true message, or if they use me only because the lighter tunes or stirring rhythms appeal to them, then they might just as well throw me in the trash heap and find something else which will really challenge and inspire them. For the men and women who have written my hymns have written them out of the deepest and holiest experiences of their lives. They have been as truly set apart by God for a holy ministry as have the heralds of the faith. In the words which they have written will be found expressed the conflicts, the sufferings, the aspirations, the victories of Christian men and women the world over. If Christians could better understand this, surely they would understand why I am so hurt and grieved when they sing my sacred words mechanically and thoughtlessly. If they only knew it, they are really only cheating themselves of some of the very highest possible moments of spiritual exaltation and communion.

I sometimes think that some congregations are cheating themselves in another way, too. Why do they use my gospel songs almost exclusively in their worship services and consistently neglect the great worship hymns which are to be found within my covers? I appreciate my gospel songs, for they speak personally to the heart of man, but too few Christians realize that they are the beginning and not the end of achievement in worship and praise, and that this beginning should be followed by growth in the art of worship. To really grow in this art, Christians must learn and use the great worship hymns of the church, for nothing can express the true spirit of worship as can one of these great hymns, such as "Come, Thou Almighty King," "All Hail the Power of Jesus' Name," or "Crown Him with Many Crowns."

Sometimes I find that even a pastor is at fault in the use he makes of me. However, I do not blame him too harshly, for he has often grown up in a church where there has been little to give him a larger knowledge or understanding of my value or correct use. But if he lacks this knowledge, how can I expect his congregation to acquire it? Just the other day, I was in a church which was observing the Lord's Supper, and the pastor selected the hymn, "Break Thou the Bread of Life," to be used as the communion hymn. I wanted so much to be able to tell him that that hymn does not refer to the "bread" which is broken in the Lord's Supper, but rather is it a prayer hymn for deeper spiritual understanding of the Scriptures which are in this case referred to as the "Bread of life." If he had only taken a little time to study the hymn, this meaning would have been evident. If pastors would only give something of the same thought and prayer to the selection of their hymns that they do to the selection of their texts and the planning of their sermons, and if only song leaders would not consider me so unimportant as to spend five minutes or less in the hasty selection of the hymns they are to lead, they might find that I could contribute far more to their service than they have imagined.

I should like to tell every pastor that he is the key to the kind of music he has in his church. It does not matter whether God has given him much talent along musical lines; the thing which really matters is that he recognize the important place which music should hold in every service, and study to show himself approved unto God in a practical working knowledge of sacred music. If he catches the vision and leads his people to catch it, too, than I can hope for a new day in the use of my sacred contents.

But it would seem that I am in a complaining mood today! However, in spite of all my abuse and misuse, there are times when I do have cause for rejoicing! When I am placed in the hands of a congregation who sings with enthusiasm and joy and worshipful spirit, I know that my God is honored, and that he, too, rejoices in the praise which rises to his waiting ears. When I find a worshiper who sings that really wonderful hymn of exultant worship and praise, "O Worship the King," with heart joyously responding to the thought that God is "our Maker, Defender, Redeemer and Friend," then I, too, know that my mission has not been in vain, and that I am fulfilling the plan and purpose which God had when he placed me in the hands of men to be used for his glory.

(Optional ending. If the following quiz is omitted, conclude with last paragraph which follows quiz.)

While I am voicing my sentiments to you today, it might be interesting to find out just how much you, as representative of an average congregation in an average church, know about the hymns and gospel songs which are contained within my pages. I am sure that many of you listen with interest to Dr. I. Q. and his famous quiz program and increase your general knowledge thereby. Then why not now listen to Dr. H. B. as he presents a quiz which will test your knowledge of hymns and increase your musical knowledge thereby? If each of you is ready with pencil and the prepared quiz sheets, I shall now give you my famous Dr. H. B. quiz entitled, "Know Your Hymns?" Ten seconds will be allowed for the answer to each question; you will find a cue to the answer in most of the questions themselves. Are you all ready? Let's go!

QUESTION No. 1—

How many of you know which of my hymns was written by a young man by the name of Ray Palmer when he was only twenty-two years of age? The year in which it was written was one of illness and poverty, but out of the deep spiritual experience which resulted, Ray Palmer looked up to Christ to strengthen his "fainting heart" and expressed his need in the prayer hymn which contains these words:

Bid darkness turn to day,
Wipe sorrow's tears away,
Nor let me ever stray
From Thee aside.

QUESTION No. 2—

How many know what hymn was inspired by the words of a man of God as he spoke to an unsaved young lady, telling her to "cut the cable and come to Jesus just as you are?"

QUESTION No. 3—

What gospel song was inspired by the following event in Christian history? In A.D. 62, Paul, a prisoner of Rome, was called into the presence of King Agrippa and Bernice to state his case. In one of his most persuasive addresses he told of his early persecution of the Christians, and of his call on the Damascus road which so transformed his life. At the close of this discourse, King Agrippa said, "Almost thou persuadest me to be a Christian," to which Paul replied: "I would to God, that not only thou, but also all that hear me this day, were both almost, and altogether such as I am, except these bonds" (Acts 26:28, 29). What gospel song did this scene inspire?

QUESTION No. 4—

Do you know which of my hymns has been declared by Matthew Arnold to be the greatest Christian hymn in the English language? It is based on Paul's words, "God forbid that I should glory, save in the cross of our Lord Jesus Christ, by whom the world is crucified unto me, and I unto the world" (Galatians 6:14); and its second stanza begins, "Forbid it, Lord, that I should boast save in the death of Christ, my God."

QUESTION No. 5—

How many of you who sing his many hymns, could tell the name of the great English hymn writer who wrote "Jesus, Lover of My Soul," "Hark, the Herald Angels Sing," and "Love Divine, All Love Excelling"? And did you know that his high calling as a hymn writer came to him out of an extraordinary experience which made the writing of religious poetry nothing less than a passion to him and resulted in the writing of over six thousand hymns during his lifetime?

QUESTION No. 6—

Do those of you who sing her many hymns know the name of the great woman hymn writer who was blind?

QUESTION No. 7—

And can you name one of the hymns which she has written?

QUESTION No. 8—

Frances Ridley Havergal is another great woman hymn writer. One day, while in a minister's study, her eyes lit upon a picture of Jesus Christ under which was written the inscription: "I did this for thee: what hast thou done for me?" As she gazed on the face of the suffering Redeemer, the lines of a poem framed themselves in her mind, and she hastily wrote them out on the back of a circular. Later, thinking them hardly worthy to save, she started to cast them into the fire, but some impulse restrained her from doing so. Later they were made into one of our well-loved hymns. How many know what hymn was inspired in this way?

QUESTION No. 9—

Did you know that it was a young Baptist ministerial student by the name of Samuel Frances Smith who wrote our American national hymn? He wrote it when he was only twenty-three years of age, composing it in less than a half hour! What is our American national hymn?

QUESTION No. 10—

Edward Hopper, while laboring among sea-faring men, wrote a hymn which spoke to these men in the familiar terms of their daily work. It is full of references to the sea and reminds one of a miracle which Christ performed one night when he and his disciples were on the Sea of Galilee. Do you know this hymn of the sea?

QUESTION No. 11—

John Fawcett was the pastor of a little Baptist church in England when he received a call to a large church in London. At first he accepted this call, but his people, with much pleading and weeping, finally prevailed upon him to sacrifice his larger ambitions and remain with them until his death. As a result of this experience, he wrote a hymn which has become a great favorite in all parts of the world, especially when a hymn expressing the unity of Christian believers is desired. Do you recognize this hymn?

QUESTION No. 12—

Katherine Lee Bates, teacher of English in Wellesley College, had spent a day on Pike's Peak with some fellow teachers, looking over the granduer and beauty of the Colorado Rockies. That evening she sat down in her room in Colorado Springs and wrote one of our greatest American hymns, expressing praise for the beauty of our land and calling on God to shed his grace on her. What is this American hymn called?

QUESTION No. 13—

The four lines which have been sung more than any other four lines in the English language were originally the last stanza to a morning and an evening hymn written by the Bishop Ken of England. What are these four lines called which you sing almost every Sunday morning?

QUESTION No. 14—

Which of my famous missionary hymns was written for a flag-raising held at a young ladies' seminary in 1848? It was sung for the first time by the young ladies themselves, and since has been sung at thousands of missionary meetings the world over.

QUESTION No. 15—

Do you know which of my hymns was the great war song of the Reformation, written by Martin Luther and sung every day by Luther and his friends? It is based on Psalm 46, which begins, "God is our refuge and strength, a very present help in trouble."

QUESTION No. 16—

One of my hymns is brought to mind by the Scripture verses which reveal that Christ is the Good Shepherd and that "all we like sheep have gone astray." What is this Shepherd hymn called?

QUESTION No. 17—

Do you know what hymn has been called a great character-making hymn because of its appeal to young people to be true, pure, strong, and brave?

QUESTION No. 18—

What hymn suggests the experiences of the Israelite people in the wilderness with its reference to "pilgrim thro' this barren land," "bread of heaven," "crystal fountain," and "fire and cloudy pillar"?

QUESTION No. 19—

Two Baptists wrote the words and the tune to one of our great consecration hymns. A cue to its title will be found in the following words from its last stanza:

> All that I am and have,
> Thy gifts so free —
> In joy, in grief, thro' life,
> Dear Lord, for Thee!

QUESTION No. 20—

What hymn is a call to the Christian to follow Christ in intimate communion and in active service? It also calls away from the "cares and pleasures" of the material life to serve and love him best of all.

QUESTION No. 21—

Do you know what great worship hymn pays homage and praise in its separate stanzas to God as "King," as the "Incarnate Word," as the "Holy Comforter," and as the "Great One in Three"?

QUESTION No. 22—

Do you know what hymn is recognized as the great "church" song of the world, suggesting the great, universal, spiritual church, built upon the foundation of Jesus Christ?

QUESTION No. 23—

One of my greatest hymns has been called a "bugle call to spiritual battle." It was written as a marching song for some school children to sing as they marched from one village to another to attend a religious festival in England. Since then hundreds of thousands of Christian soldiers of the cross have marched to its stirring tempo. What is the title of this hymn?

QUESTION No. 24—

Ernest Shurtleff was asked by his fellow ministerial classmates to write a hymn that they might sing together at their graduation from the theological seminary which they were attending. For this occasion he produced the hymn which expresses the church militant spirit for young ministers starting out on their life's career, suggesting as it does that "the day of march has come." I wonder how many young ministers as well as young Christians know this stirring hymn of conquest?

QUESTION No. 25—

One of the greatest hymns of the church militant was written by Bishop Heber as he had a vision of Christ's great army growing from the small company of 120 in the upper room to a host of millions of followers the world over. It was not an army with spears and swords but with "blood-red banners" that he pictured, being led by the Son of God, and calling to Christians everywhere to follow in his train. Do you know this hymn of spiritual conquest?

This concludes our quiz. Even if you haven't found all the answers, I hope that this quiz has awakened a little more enthusiasm on your part to sing with the spirit and with the understanding also when you sing from my pages in future years.

I hope, too, that because I, Dr. Hymnbook, have talked to you today, you will no longer think of me as a passing acquaintance or a tolerated fixture in the services in which you use me, but that you will now recognize me as your friend in worship and your co-worker in building God's kingdom upon earth!

ANSWERS TO "DR. H. B." QUIZ

1. My Faith Looks Up to Thee

2. Just As I Am

3. Almost Persuaded

4. When I Survey the Wondrous Cross

5. Charles Wesley

6. Fanny Crosby

7. All the Way My Saviour Leads Me; Blessed Assurance; Close To Thee; I Am Thine, O Lord; Near the Cross; Pass Me Not; Praise Him! Praise Him!; Rescue the Perishing; Safe in the Arms of Jesus, etc.

8. I Gave My Life for Thee

9. America

10. Jesus, Saviour, Pilot Me

11. Blest Be the Tie

12. America the Beautiful

13. Doxology

14. Fling Out the Banner

15. A Mighty Fortress Is Our God

16. Saviour, Like a Shepherd Lead Us

17. I Would Be True

18. Guide Me, O Thou Great Jehovah

19. Something for Thee

20. Jesus Calls Us

21. Come, Thou Almighty King

22. The Church's One Foundation

23. Onward, Christian Soldiers

24. Lead On, O King Eternal

25. The Son of God Goes Forth to War

APPENDIXES

APPENDIX I

SOURCES OF HYMNS USED

CODE FOR HYMNALS: (Numbers under code letter refer to number of hymn in each hymnal.)

    *Am—American Hymnal (Baptist)

    *Br—Broadman Hymnal (Baptist)

    Cw—Christian Worship (Baptist and Disciples)

    Cy—Christian Youth Hymnal (Lutheran)

    Fa—Favorite Hymns (Christian)

    Me—Methodist Hymnal

    *Mo—Modern Hymnal (Baptist)

    *Nb—New Baptist Hymnal

    Pi—Pilgrim Hymnal (Congregational)

    Pr—The Hymnal (Presbyterian U. S. A.)

    *Vp—Voice of Praise (Baptist)

EXPLANATION OF CODE:

The hymn, "Abide with Me," is used on p. 211 of this book. It will be found in the American Hymnal (Am), No. 209; the Broadman Hymnal (Br), No. 179; Christian Worship (Cw), No. 138; Christian Youth Hymnal (Cy), No. 128; Favorite Hymns (Fa), No. 230; etc.

---

*—Published by Broadman Press

Come, Thou Fount of Every Blessing, pp. 36, 169—Am 247, Br 190, Cw 111, Fa 212, Me 23, Mo 104, Nb 223, Pr 235, Vp 190.

Crossing the Bar, p. 65—Cw 574, Me 368, Nb 290, Pi 436, Pr 438.

Crown Him with Many Crowns, pp. 110, 215—Am 3, Br 18, Cw 250, Cy 59, Me 170, Mo 5, Nb 141, Pr 190, Vp 1.

Dare to Be Brave, Dare to Be True, pp. 82, 151—Br 320, Nb 401.

Day Is Dying in the West, pp. 203, 211—Am 35, Br 87, Cw 144, Cy 125, Fa 291, Me 44, Mo 39, Nb 12, Pi 66, Pr 39, Vp 130.

Dear Lord and Father of Mankind, pp. 45, 80, 200, 211—Br 401, Cw 411, Cy 215, Me 342, Nb 63, Pi 224, Pr 302.

Did You Think to Pray?, pp. 27, 158, 159—Am 218, Br 335, Fa 217.

Face to Face, pp. 16, 78—Am 281, Br 106, Fa 82, Mo 41, Nb 390.

Fairest Lord Jesus, pp. 38, 106, 207—Am 157, Br 211, Cw 261, Cy 82, Fa 226, Me 111, Mo 68, Nb 102, Pi 465, Pr 194, Vp 215.

Faith Is the Victory, p. 23—Mo 314, Nb 355, Vp 14.

Faith of Our Fathers, pp. 154, 211—Am 418, Br 201, Cw 348, Cy 212, Fa 232, Me 256, Mo 172, Nb 249, Pi 220, Pr 267, Vp 201.

Faith of Our Mothers, p. 136—Br 203, Vp 203.

Fight the Good Fight, p. 56—Am 514, Br 270, Cw 376, Cy 204, Me 286, Mo 475, Nb 200, Pi 255, Pr 270.

Fling Out the Banner, pp. 210, 222—Am 224, Br 152, Cw 540, Cy 271, Fa 219, Me 502, Mo 96, Nb 258, Pi 371, Pr 384, Vp 152.

Footsteps of Jesus, pp. 52, 199—Am 143, Br 228, Mo 397, Vp 222.

For the Beauty of the Earth, pp. 39, 70, 169, 204—Am 86, Br 246, Cw 167, Cy 184, Me 18, Mo 199, Nb 309, Pi 168, Pr 71, Vp 213.

Forward Through the Ages, p. 56—Br 419, Cw 498, Pi 400.

From Every Stormy Wind That Blows, p. 211—Am 246, Br 189, Cw 394, Fa 273, Me 317, Mo 103, Nb 185, Pi 480, Vp 189.

Give of Your Best to the Master, pp. 93, 202—Am 50, Br 366, Cy 242, Fa 149, Mo 329, Nb 375, Vp 286.

Glorious Things of Thee Are Spoken, p. 90—Am 229, Cw 431, Fa 286, Me 382, Mo 92, Nb 241, Pi 405, Pr 339.

God of Our Fathers, Known of Old, p. 153—Am 519, Br 224, Cw 560, 561, Me 491, Mo 479, Nb 304, Pi 383.

God of Our Fathers, Whose Almighty Hand, p. 35—Am 512, Br 240, Cw 551, Cy 163, Me 496, Mo 473, Nb 26, Pi 356, Pr 414.

God Will Take Care of You, pp. 6, 128, 142, 194-196—Am 37, Fa 86, Mo 247, Nb 366.

Guide Me, O Thou Great Jehovah, pp. 4, 222—Am 235, Br 181, Cw 393, Fa 266, Me 301, Mo 71, Nb 43, Pr 104, Vp 181.

Hark, Ten Thousand Harps and Voices, p. 109—Am 250, Br 227, Cw 268, Me 167, Mo 98, Nb 130.

Hark, the Herald Angels Sing, pp. 173, 174, 217—Am 72, Br 142, Cw 189, Cy 12, Me 86, Mo 404, Nb 83, Pi 91, Pr 117, Vp 142.

Lord, Lay Some Soul upon My Heart, p. 160—Br 451, Vp 238.

Lord, Speak to Me That I May Speak, pp. 5, 115—Am 216, Cw 470, Cy 260, Me 460, Mo 184, Nb 211, Pi 339, Pr 399.

Love Divine, All Love Excelling, pp. 74, 217—Am 10, Br 19, Cw 379, Cy 77, Fa 283, Me 372, Mo 10, Nb 183, Pi 270, Pr 308, Vp 4.

Love Lifted Me, p. 210—Am 353, Br 352, Fa 61, Mo 333, Vp 55.

Loyalty to Christ, p. 153—Am 302, Br 374, Mo 285.

Majestic Sweetness Sits Enthroned, pp. 18, 102, 103, 105, 108—Am 117, Br 188, Cw 381, Fa 243, Me 220, Mo 81, Nb 132, Pi 490, Pr 197, Vp 170.

Make Me a Channel of Blessing, pp. 26, 202—Am 320, Br 61, Mo 261, Vp 27.

Master, No Offering Costly and Sweet, p. 81—Cw 303, Me 464, Nb 214, Pi 334, Pr 407.

Moment by Moment, p. 6—Am 43, Br 58, Mo 274.

More About Jesus, p. 5—Fa 259, Mo 168, Nb 324, Vp 169.

More Like the Master, p. 78—Fa 119, Mo 360.

More Love to Thee, O Christ, pp. 21, 80, 199, 200, 214—Am 220, Br 218, Cw 390, Fa 208, Me 364, Mo 379, Nb 195, Pi 146, Pr 315, Vp 227.

Must Jesus Bear the Cross Alone?, p. 131—Am 198, Br 153, Cw 366, Fa 254, Me 276, Mo 106, Nb 204, Vp 154.

My Faith Looks Up to Thee, pp. 60, 76, 211, 221—Am 107, Br 209, Cw 355, Cy 200, Fa 213, Me 213, Mo 159, Nb 168, Pi 498, Pr 285, Vp 198.

My Hope Is Built on Nothing Less, p. 99—Am 34, Br 96, Me 244, Mo 38, Nb 362, Vp 22.

My Jesus, As Thou Wilt, p. 63—Am 208, Br 178, Cw 408, Me 330, Mo 77, Nb 222, Pi 494, Pr 280, Vp 178.

My Jesus, I Love Thee, p. 144—Am 105, Br 154, Cw 382, Fa 203, Me 234, Mo 157, Nb 323, Pi 509, Vp 261.

My Prayer, p. 81—Am 139, Br 217, Fa 265, Mo 152, Vp 226.

My Redeemer, p. 107—Br 388, Fa 121, Vp 106.

My Soul, Be on Thy Guard, p. 82—Am 201, Br 247, Cw 370, Cy 223, Fa 201, Me 277, Mo 88, Nb 177, Pi 256, Vp 174.

Near the Cross, p. 210—Am 484, Br 294, Cw 339, Cy 27, Fa 250, Me 248, Mo 239, Nb 350, Vp 156.

Near to the Heart of God, pp. 45, 100 (See "The Heart of God"—App. II) —Br 273, Vp 225.

Nothing Between, p. 158—Am 482, Br 66, Mo 227.

Now in the Days of Youth, pp. 7, 38—Cw 300, Cy 240, Pi 477.

Now the Day Is Over, pp. 72, 207—Am 146, Br 194, Cw 149, Cy 132, Fa 292, Me 53, Mo 141, Nb 15, Pi 58, Pr 35.

O Brother Man, Fold to Thy Heart Thy Brother, pp. 75, 81—Br 403, Cw 515, Cy 280, Me 466, Nb 275, Pi 310, Pr 403.

O Church of God, p. 86—Cw 432.

O Come, All Ye Faithful, pp. 172, 173, 179—Am 152, Br 143, Cw 205, Cy 7, Me 96, Mo 46, Nb 90, Pi 105, Pr 116, Vp 143.

O Come, O Come, Emmanuel, pp. 179, 186 (See Appendix II)—Cw 182, Cy 4, Me 83, Pi 69, Pr 108.

O Day of Rest and Gladness, p. 159—Am 4, Br 11, Cw 443, Cy 111, Fa 4, Me 396, Mo 4, Nb 8, Pi 31, Pr 18, Vp 129.

O for a Faith That Will Not Shrink, pp. 76, 81—Am 231, Br 277, Me 270, Nb 62, Pi 223, Vp 269.

O for a Thousand Tongues to Sing, pp. 170, 198, 214—Am 266, Br 5, Cw 262, Me 162, Mo 182, Nb 128, Pr 199, Vp 125.

O God, Our Help in Ages Past, pp. 33, 196, 197—Am 160, Br 435, Cw 585, Cy 56, Me 533, Mo 173, Nb 39, Pi 177, Pr 77, Vp 193.

O God, We Pray for All Mankind, pp. 68, 165, 166—Nb 267.

O Happy Day, pp. 157, 158, 198—Am 134, Br 461, Fa 214, Me 212, Mo 43, Nb 251, Vp 294.

O Holy Night, p. 179 (See Appendix II)—Br 468.

O Jesus, I Have Promised, p. 98—Am 205, Br 187, Cw 308, Cy 241, Me 226, Mo 80, Nb 193, Pi 196, Pr 268, Vp 195.

O Jesus, Thou Art Standing, pp. 94, 153, 204, 207, 211—Am 244, Br 242, Cw 279, Cy 210, Fa 245, Me 197, Mo 101, Nb 179, Pi 246, Pr 228.

O Little Town of Bethlehem, pp. 174, 175, 183—Am 114, Br 144, Cw 184, Cy 14, Fa 151, Me 100, Mo 406, Nb 82, Pi 74, Pr 121, Vp 144.

O Love That Wilt Not Let Me Go, pp. 51, 147, 202—Am 120, Br 231, Cw 388, Cy 202, Fa 268, Me 318, Mo 439, Nb 232, Pi 289, Pr 307, Vp 219.

O Master, Let Me Walk with Thee, pp. 26, 75, 160, 202—Am 254, Br 202, Cw 307, Cy 195, Fa 207, Me 259, Mo 149, Nb 274, Pi 291, Pr 364, Vp 202.

O Master Workman of the Race, p. 95—Cw 210, Me 118, Pi 328, Pr 140.

Only Trust Him, p. 198—Am 104, Br 197, Me 184, Mo 165, Nb 331, Vp 197.

Onward, Christian Soldiers, p. 222—Am 31, Br 46, Cw 482, Cy 232, Fa 300, Me 280, Mo 35, Nb 209, Pi 399, Pr 365, Vp 9.

Open My Eyes, That I May See, pp. 100, 112, 113, 114, 115—Am 457, Br 351, Fa 145.

Our Best, pp. 100, 202—Am 361, Br 343, Mo 342, Vp 87.

O Word of God Incarnate, pp. 88, 92, 148—Br 75, Cw 434, Cy 138, Me 386, Nb 75, Pi 421, Pr 215.

O Worship the King, pp. 87, 170, 216—Am 118, Br 2, Cw 94, Cy 85, Fa 263, Me 4, Mo 1, Nb 34, Pi 5, Pr 2, Vp 122.

O Zion, Haste, p. 211—Am 223, Br 151, Cw 529, Cy 266, Me 475, Mo 95, Nb 264, Pi 372, Pr 382, Vp 151.

Pass Me Not, O Gentle Saviour, pp. 81, 199—Am 425, Br 230, Me 231, Mo 311, Nb 349, Vp 224.

Praise God from Whom All Blessings Flow (Doxology), pp. 141, 169, 222—Am 531, Br 481, Cw 611, Cy 339, Fa 309, Me 616, Mo 483, Nb 408, Pi 518, Pr 503, Vp 300.

Praise Him! Praise Him!, pp. 43, 47, 170—Am 65, Br 355, Fa 3, Mo 393, Nb 326, Vp 2.

Purer in Heart, O God, p. 75—Br 272, Cw 343.

Rejoice, Ye Pure in Heart, p. 170—Br 285, Cw 418, Cy 87, Me 358, Nb 47, Pi 476, Pr 297.

The First Noel, p. 183—Br 140, Cw 197, Cy 15, Me 97, Pi 97, Pr 129.

The Great Physician, p. 29—Am 423, Br 226, Mo 367, Vp 267.

The King of Love My Shepherd Is, p. 211—Am 516, Cw 169, Cy 193, Nb 224, Pi 287, Pr 99.

The Light of the World Is Jesus, pp. 15, 142, 145, 146, 147—Am 389, Br 330, Vp 230.

The Lord Is My Shepherd, pp. 15, 44, 46, 47, 170—Br 22, Cw 170, Fa 279, Nb 66, Vp 67.

The Nail-Scarred Hand, p. 30—Am 296, Br 397, Mo 291, Vp 39.

The Old Rugged Cross, pp. 54, 130, 210, 211—Am 324, Br 71, Fa 9, Mo 279, Nb 369, Vp 34.

There's a Song in the Air, pp. 186, 187 (See Appendix II)—Cw 198, Me 98, Pi 82.

There Is a Green Hill Far Away, pp. 104, 203—Am 268, Br 98, Cw 230, Cy 33, Me 135, Mo 36, Nb 106, Pi 121, Pr 157, Vp 98.

The Son of God Goes Forth to War, pp. 23, 53, 54, 55, 222—Am 18, Br 21, Cw 358, Cy 219, Fa 236, Me 285, Mo 8, Nb 198, Pi 377, Pr 271, Vp 65.

The Star-Spangled Banner, p. 154—Am 518, Br 457, Fa 303, Mo 478, Nb 303, Pi 357.

The Way of the Cross, p. 180—Am 359, Fa 167, Mo 347.

This Is My Father's World, pp. 39, 169—Am 54, Cw 171, Cy 180, Fa 146, Me 72, Mo 54, Nb 406, Pi 464, Pr 70.

Thou Didst Leave Thy Throne, p. 179—Am 22, Br 138, Cw 292, Cy 6, Me 95, Nb 123, Pr 231.

Thy Word Have I Hid in My Heart, pp. 148, 158—Am 316, Br 389, Mo 297, Vp 107.

'Tis So Sweet to Trust in Jesus, p. 140—Br 284, Fa 183, Mo 363, Nb 322, Vp 249.

'Tis the Blessed Hour of Prayer, p. 88—Am 45, Br 156, Cw 332, Fa 248, Mo 258, Vp 43.

To the Work, p. 202—Am 74, Br 64, Fa 32, Mo 49, Vp 53.

Touch Me, Lord Jesus, p. 31—Br 463.

Tread Softly, pp. 14, 156, 157—Br 485, Mo 443, Vp 305.

Watchman, Tell Us of the Night, pp. 204, 210—Am 520, Cw 183, Me 485, Nb 263, Pi 70, Pr 109.

We've a Story to Tell to the Nations, pp. 164, 165—Am 70, Br 379, Cw 530, Cy 268, Fa 44, Me 501, Mo 312, Nb 261, Pi 374, Vp 7.

We Would See Jesus, p. 73—Am 193, Br 220, Cw 400, Mo 134, Nb 219, Pi 506, Pr 263.

What a Friend, pp. 6, 60, 207—Am 238, Br 160, Cw 331, Cy 185, Fa 252, Me 240, Mo 119, Nb 319, Pi 478, Pr 257, Vp 160.

When I Survey the Wondrous Cross, pp. 54, 77, 131, 211, 221—Am 262, Br 191, Cw 228, Cy 36, Fa 272, Me 148, Mo 105, Nb 108, Pi 122, Pr 152, Vp 191.

Appendix II

SOURCES OF OTHER MUSIC MATERIALS USED

An Evening Prayer—Charles H. Gabriel; in *Rodeheaver's Low Voice Collection No. 1*, and *Rodeheaver's High Voice Collection No. 2*; Publisher, Rodeheaver, Hall-Mack Co.

Beside Still Waters—Bernard Hamblen; Arrangements, Solo for High and Low Voice; SA; SATB; Publisher, Boosey, Hawkes, Inc.

Christmas Carolers' Book in Song and Story—Torstein O. Kvamme; Publisher, Hall & McCreary Co.

Christ Went Up into the Hills—Richard Hageman; Arrangements, Solo for High and Low Voice; SATB; Publisher, C. Fischer.

Cross, The—Harriet Ware; Arrangement, Solo for High and Low Voice; Publisher, G. Schirmer.

Crusader's Hymn (Beautiful Saviour)—Melody of 12th Century, arr. by Frederick Wick; Arrangement, SATB; Publisher, Frederick Wick.

Good Shepherd, The—Beardsley Van de Water; Arrangements, Solo for High and Low Voice; SATB; Publisher, Oliver Ditson.

Green Pastures—Wilfred Sanderson; Arrangement, Solo for High and Low Voice; Publisher, Boosey, Hawkes, Inc.

Hallelujah Chorus—The Messiah—George Frederick Handel; in any edition of *The Messiah*; *Broadman Hymnal*, No. 477.

Heart of God, The (Near to the Heart of God)—C. B. McAfee; Arrangements, Unison or 2-part; SSA; SATB; Publisher, Lorenz. See Appendix I.

He Shall Feed His Flock—The Messiah—George Frederick Handel; in any edition of *The Messiah*; in "Everybody's Favorite Wedding and Sacred Music for the Organ" (Hammond Registration); Publisher, Amsco.

How Beautiful upon the Mountains—J. Stainer; in *The Church Chorister*; Publisher, Hall & McCreary Co.

I'd Rather Have Jesus—Beverly Shea; Arrangements, Solo and Male Quartet—Publisher, Moody Press; Male Chorus or Quartet, arr. by Jones—Publisher, Rodeheaver, Hall-Mack Co.

I'll Take My Staff and Travel On (White Spiritual)—arr. by R. Deane Shure; Arrangement, SATB; Publisher, Belwin, Inc.

Into the Woods My Master Went—George B. Nevin; Arrangements, Solo for High and Low Voice; SATB; Publisher, Oliver Ditson.

I Will Lift Up Mine Eyes—F. Flaxington Harker; Arrangements, Solo for High and Low Voice; SATB; Publisher, Harold Flammer.

I Will Lift Up Mine Eyes—Alfred Wooler; Arrangement, Solo for High, Medium, and Low Voice; Publisher, Boosey, Hawkes, Inc.

Just for Today—Jane Bingham Abbott; Arrangements, Solo for High and Low Voice; Duet for High and Low Voices; Publisher, C. F. Summy.

King of Love My Shepherd Is, The—Harry Rowe Shelley; Arrangements, Solo for Mezzo Soprano or Baritone; Duet for High and Low Voices; SATB with Alto Solo; TTBB; SSA; Publisher, G. Schirmer.

Led By a Star (Christmas Cantata)—Text, J. Lilian Vandevere; Music, Haydn M. Morgan; Arrangement, SATB (Chorus parts and accompaniment edition published separately); Publisher, C. C. Birchard.

Lift Up Your Heads—James H. Rogers; Arrangement, SATB; Publisher, G. Schirmer.

Lift Up Your Heads—E. L. Ashford; Arrangements, SATB; SSA; Publisher, Lorenz.

Lift Up Your Heads—B. B. McKinney; Arrangement, Unison (in Music Supplement to the Vacation Bible School Joint Service Book); Publisher, Broadman Press.

Lord Bless You and Keep You, The (Farewell Anthem with Sevenfold Amen) —Peter C. Lutkin; Arrangement, SATB; Publisher, C. F. Summy.

Mountains—Oscar Rasbach; Arrangements, Solo for High and Medium Voice; SATB; SSA; TTBB; Publisher, G. Schirmer.

My Task—E. L. Ashford; Arrangements, Solo in five keys SATB; SSA; SA; TTBB; Publisher, Lorenz.

O Come, All Ye Faithful (Adeste Fidelis)—John Reading, arr. by Vincent Novello; Arrangement, SATB (Sop. and Ten. Solos, Alto, Ten. and Bass Trio, Ten. and Bass Duet, and Mixed Voices); Publisher, Oliver Ditson.

O Come, O Come, Emmanuel—Christmas Hymns Set IV; Adaptations by Roy Ringwald and Robert Shaw (also includes O Little Town of Bethlehem and Silent Night); Waring Mixed Chorus Series; Publisher, Words & Music. See Appendix I.

O God, We Thank Thee—Barnes; Arrangement, SATB; Publisher, H. T. Fitzsimmons.

O Holy Night (Cantique de Noel)—Adolphe Adam; in *Christmas Carols and Choruses;* Publisher, Hall & McCreary Co. See Appendix I.

On a Hill (A Spiritual)—Lola Gibson Deaton; Arrangements, Solo for High and Low Voice; TTBB; SSA; SATB; Publisher, G. Schirmer.

Onward, Christian Soldiers—arr. by Harry Simeone; Waring Mixed Chorus Series; Publisher, Shawnee Press.

Soft Were Your Hands, Dear Jesus—Geoffrey O'Hara; Arrangement, Solo for High, Medium, and Low Voice; Publisher, Willis Music Co. (Huntzinger)

Silent Night—Gruber, arr. by Wetzel; Arrangement, SATB; Antiphonal Arrangement; Publisher, Gamble Hinged Music Co.

Stranger of Galilee, The—Mrs. C. H. Morris; in *Rodeheaver Gospel Solos and Duets, No. 1;* Publisher, Rodeheaver, Hall-Mack Co.

Stranger of Galilee, The—Morris, arr. by Treharne; Arrangements, Solo for High, Medium, and Low Voice; SATB; Publisher, Boston Music Co.

Take Up Thy Cross—A. H. Ackley; in *Rodeheaver Gospel Solos and Duets, No. 1;* Publisher, Rodeheaver, Hall-Mack Co.

There's a Song in the Air—Oley Speaks, arr. by Carl Deis; Arrangements, SSA; SATB; Publisher, G. Schirmer. See Appendix I.

Trust in Him—Bernard Hamblen; Arrangements, Solo for High and Low Voice; SATB; Publisher, G. Schirmer.

Twenty-Third Psalm, The—Albert Hay Malotte; Arrangements, Solo for High, Medium, and Low Voice; SSA; SATB; Publisher, G. Schirmer.

Were You There? (Spiritual)—H. T. Burleigh; Arrangements, Solo for High, Medium, and Low Voice; SATB; Simplified Arrangement; Publisher, G. Ricordi.

Were You There? (Spiritual)—arr. by Roy Ringwald; Waring Mixed Chorus Series; Publisher, Shawnee Press.

Were You There? (Spiritual)—arr. by Roger C. Wilson; Arrangement, SATB; Publisher, Lorenz.

You Taught Me How to Pray—Helen Jun Marth; Arrangements, SSA; SATB; Publisher, Edwin H. Morris.

Appendix III

PUBLISHERS OF MATERIALS USED

MUSIC PUBLISHERS

Amsco Publishing Co., 1600 Broadway, New York 19, N. Y.
Augsburg Publishing Co., Minneapolis, Minn.
C. C. Birchard & Co., 285 Columbus Ave., Boston 16, Mass.
Belwin, Inc., 43 West 23rd Street, New York 10, N. Y.
Boosey, Hawkes, Inc., 43-47 West 23rd Street, New York 10, N. Y.
Boston Music., 116 Boylston Street, Boston 16, Mass.
Broadman Press, 161 Eighth Ave., North, Nashville 3, Tenn.
Chappell & Co., R. K. O. Building, Rockefeller Center, New York, N. Y.
Oliver Ditson Co., Bryn Mawr, Pa.
    (Theodore Presser, Distributors)
Carl Fischer, Inc., 62 Cooper Square, New York, N. Y.
H. T. Fitzsimmons Co., Inc., 615 N. LaSalle Street, Chicago 10, Ill.
Harold Flammer, Inc., 251 West 19th Street, New York 11, N. Y.
Gamble Hinged Music Co., 218 S. Wabash Ave., Chicago 5, Ill.
Hall & McCreary Co., 434 S. Wabash Ave., Chicago 5, Ill.
Raymond L. Hoffman Co., 118 West Ohio Street, Chicago 10, Ill.
Neil A. Kjos Music Co., 223 West Lake Street, Chicago 6, Ill.
Lorenz Publishing Co., 501 E. 3rd Street, Dayton 1, Ohio
Mills Music Co., 1619 Broadway, New York, N. Y.
Moody Press, 153 Institute Place, Chicago 10, Ill.
Edwin H. Morris Co., Inc., 549 W. 52nd Street, New York 19, N. Y.
G. Ricordi & Co., New York, N. Y.
Rodeheaver Hall-Mack Co., Winona Lake, Ind.
Shawnee Press, Inc., 1697 Broadway, New York 19, N. Y.
G. Schirmer, Inc., 3 East 43rd Street, New York 17, N. Y.
Clayton F. Summy Co., 321 South Wabash Ave., Chicago 4, Ill.
Frederick Wick, Minneapolis, Minn.

Willis Music Co., 137 W. 4th Street, Cincinnati, Ohio
    (Agents for R. L. Huntzinger)
B. F. Wood Music Co., 88 St. Stephens Street, Boston, Mass.
Words & Music, Inc. (See Shawnee Press)

BOOK PUBLISHERS

Abingdon-Cokesbury Press, 810 Broadway, Nashville, Tenn.
American Sunday School Union, 1816 Chestnut Street, Philadelphia, Pa.
Association Press, 347 Madison Ave., New York 17, N. Y.
Walter H. Baker Co., 178 Tremont Street, Boston 11, Mass.
Broadman Press (See Music Publishers)
Eldridge Entertainment House, Franklin, Ohio (or Denver 2, Colo.)
Harper & Brothers, 49 East 33rd Street, New York 16, N. Y.
Lorenz Publishing Co. (See Music Publishers)
Moody Press (See Music Publishers)
Fleming R. Revell Co., 158 Fifth Ave., New York 10, N. Y.
Rodeheaver Hall-Mack Co. (See Music Publishers)
John Rudin & Co., Inc., 1018 South Wabash Ave., Chicago, Ill.
W. A. Wilde Co., 131 Clarendon Street, Boston 16, Mass.
Zondervan Publishing Co., 847 Ottawa Avenue, N. W., Grand Rapids 2, Mich.